THE VEGAN DIET

Also by David Scott

Middle Eastern Vegetarian Cookery
Indonesian Cookery
Taste of Thailand
The Penniless Vegetarian
Protein-Rich Vegetarian Cookery

THE VEGAN DIET
TRUE VEGETARIAN
COOKERY

DAVID SCOTT &
CLAIRE GOLDING

Illustrated by Steve Hardstaff

RIDER
LONDON • SYDNEY • AUCKLAND • JOHANNESBURG

Contents

Introduction

The vegan diet consists solely of foods produced from plants, our primary food source. It does not include foods such as meat, fish or dairy products, which are secondary in the food chain.

There are three main reasons for following this diet. First, by following a vegan diet we cease contributing to the exploitation and cruelty suffered by animals reared for their flesh and products. This reason is particularly relevant now that such suffering has become an intrinsic, if not intended, part of modern factory-farming methods. Second, we benefit nutritionally because the naturally balanced food we eat, so long as it is not refined, is low in fats and cholesterol and not over-rich in protein. Further, plant food does not contain the chemicals that are fed to animals to ensure that their flesh is of the right colour and tenderness, at the right time, for the market place, thus ensuring the optimum yield per unit according to the amount of money invested. Third, the vegan diet contributes to a better use of the land available for growing food. Animal farming is an extravagant and ecologically unsound use of our resources. Many of the world's food problems could be alleviated if land devoted to animal rearing was turned over to plant-food cultivation.

Obviously, many factors are involved in choosing a vegan diet but one is particularly interesting. In a recent examination of life expectancy around the world, it was found that people who traditionally subsist on a plant-food diet, e.g. Russian Caucasians and Hunzakuts in Pakistan, came top of the 'longevity' list while those who were dependent on a meat-rich diet, e.g. Eskimos and Laplanders, came bottom.

The recipes in this book show how you can make tasty, nutritionally sound and visually attractive meals containing no animal products. They are also planned to give you ideas for embarking on your own culinary adventures in which all the ingredients are primary food sources. The book will, we hope, be useful both to practising vegans and to those people, including omnivarians and lacto-vegetarians, who wish to reduce the amount of animal foodstuffs in their diet.

The authors do not intend this book to be part of a crusade for veganism. We do, however, want to show with this collection of recipes how the vegan diet can be a complete or partial alternative to a meat-rich or to a lacto-vegetarian diet. We also give a brief résumé of the moral, ecological and nutritional arguments for the vegan diet. For the reader who wishes to investigate these areas more deeply, we have given a bibliography at the back of the book. For a complete, lucid and authoritative synopsis of the arguments for a vegetarian diet (with a chapter on veganism) see *Food for a Future* by Jon Wynne-Tyson.

The Vegan's Moral Case
Arguments ancient and modern

Many famous thinkers have made powerful humanitarian or ethical arguments for a diet that contains no flesh foods; rather than try to emulate them we offer here a selection of quotations. These are drawn from the excellent collections in *A Buddhist Case for Vegetarianism* by Roshi Philip Kapleau and *Food for a Future* by Jon Wynne-Tyson.

We manage to swallow flesh only because we do not think of the cruel and sinful thing we do. There are many crimes which are the creation of man himself, the wrongfulness of which is put down to his divergence from habit, custom, or tradition. But cruelty is not of these. It is a fundamental sin, and admits of no arguments or nice distinctions. If only we do not allow our heart to grow callous it protects against cruelty, is always clearly heard; and yet we go on perpetrating cruelties easily, merrily, all of us – in fact, any one who does not join in is dubbed a crank. . . . If, after our pity is aroused, we persist in throttling our feelings simply in order to join others in preying upon life, we insult all that is good in us. I have decided to try a vegetarian diet.

Rabindranath Tagore
(1861–1941)

To avoid causing terror to living beings, let the Disciple refrain from eating meat . . . the food of the wise is that which is consumed by the Sadhus [Yogis]; it does not consist of meat . . . there may be some foolish people in the future who will say that I have permitted meat-eating and that I partook of meat myself but . . . meat-eating I have not permitted to anyone, I do not permit, I will not permit . . . meat-eating in any form, in any manner, and at any place, is unconditionally and once and for all prohibited for all.

Buddha
(about 500 BC)

Slowly in our European thought comes the notion that ethics has not only to do with mankind but with animal creation as well. This begins with St Francis of Assisi. The explanation which applies only to man must be given up. Thus we shall arrive at saying that ethics is reverence for all life.

Wherever any animal is forced into the service of man the sufferings which it has to bear on that account are the concern of every one of us. No one ought to permit, in so far as he can prevent it, pain or suffering for which he will not take the responsibility. No one ought to rest at ease in the thought that in so doing he would mix himself up in affairs which are not his business. Let no one shirk the burden of his responsibility. When there is so much maltreatment of animals, when the cries of thirsting creatures go up unnoticed from the railway trucks, when there is so much roughness in our slaughterhouses, when in our kitchens so many animals suffer horrible deaths from unskilled hands, when animals endure unheard-of agonies from heartless men, or are delivered to the dreadful play of children, then we are all guilty and must bear the blame.

Albert Schweitzer
(1875–1965)

If true, the Pythagorean principles as to abstaining from flesh foster innocence; if ill-founded they at least teach us frugality, and what loss have you in losing your cruelty? I merely deprive you of the food of lions and vultures. We shall recover our sound reason only if we shall separate ourselves from the herd – the very fact of the approbation of the multitude is a proof of the unsoundness of the opinion or practice. Let us ask what is best, not what is customary. Let us love temperance – let us be just – let us refrain from bloodshed.

Seneca
(*c.* 4 BC–*c.* AD 65)

This is dreadful! Not the suffering and death of the animals, but that man suppresses in himself, unnecessarily, the highest spiritual capacity – that of sympathy and pity towards living creatures like himself – and by violating his own feelings becomes cruel. And how deeply seated in the human heart is the injunction not to take life!

Leo Tolstoy
(1828–1910)

For purely economic reasons many human beings gave up eating the flesh of animals when the Ice Ages ended, but recently the industrialization of the food industry has enabled animal foods, previously the privilege of only the rich, to be eaten daily by the average man, and so modern man has literally eaten his way back to the Ice Ages through the carcases of beasts. As the cause of mental and physical sin, no wonder meat stands out with the redness of blood. Man pays for the sin of unnecessary slaughter by the slaughter of his own kin; the revenge for the horror of the slaughterhouses is the battlefield.

Frank Wilson
(see Bibliography)

If 'rights' exist at all – and both feelings and usage indubitably prove that they do exist – they cannot be consistently awarded to men and denied to animals, since the same senses of justice and compassion apply in both cases. 'Pain is pain,' says Humphrey Primatt, 'whether it be inflicted on man or on beast: and the creature that suffers it, whether man or beast, being sensible to the misery of it while it lasts suffers evil; and the sufferance of evil, unmeritedly, unprovokedly, where no offence has been given, and no good can possibly be answered by it, but merely to exhibit power to gratify malice, is cruelty and injustice in him that occasions it.'

Henry Salt
(1851–1939)

Granted that any practice causes more pain to animals than it gives pleasure to man; is that practice moral or immoral? And if, exactly in proportion as human beings raise their heads out of the slough of selfishness, they do not with one voice answer 'Immoral', let the morality of the principle of utility be forever condemned.

John Stuart Mill
(1806–73)

It is a vulgar error to regard meat in any form as necessary to life. All that is necessary to the human body can be supplied by the vegetable kingdom. It must be admitted as a fact beyond all question that some persons are stronger and more healthy who live on that [vegetarian] food. I know how much of the prevailing meat diet is not merely a wasteful extravagance but a source of serious evil to the consumer. I have been compelled by facts to accept the conclusion that more physical evil accrues to man from erroneous habits of diet than from even alcoholic drink.

Sir Henry Thompson MD FRCS
(1820–1904)

Cruelty to animals in modern factory farming

Most modern farms rearing animals for their flesh and milk or eggs use factory assembly-line methods. The farmer/businessman comes to view the animals only as commodities to be treated and thought of as inanimate objects with no feelings or capacity to suffer pain. Their guiding principle is an economic one in which the aim is to produce most efficiently the type of meat most wanted in the market place. That this, for instance, may mean that a calf is fed a diet so inadequate that its legs lose the strength to hold it up is of no consequence. Such a system leaves no room for compassion for the animals. The literal torture they undergo in both rearing and butchering is not considered important or, perhaps, if we wish to be more charitable, not even thought about.

This is not the right book to give details of the conditions under which factory-farm animals are kept or of the processes they are subjected to, the foods they are fed or the way they are transported and finally killed, but if you wish to give more thought to these matters see *Animal Liberation* by Peter Singer.

The case against dairy products

The vegan differs from the usual definition of a vegetarian in that he or she does not eat milk, cheese, butter or eggs, or foods that contain them. Both parties share the same concern over the treatment of animals, the environment, nutrition and man's spiritual welfare, but vegans convincingly argue that it is impossible to produce eggs, milk or dairy products without subjecting the chickens and cows to the same cruelties involved in other aspects of animal farming. In this they are correct since the beef and poultry industries are inextricably linked with the milk and egg producers. The calves necessarily produced by the cows to keep them in milk end up at the slaughterhouse as do the hens that no longer lay enough eggs and the male chicks.

The Vegan Diet and Ecology

Fred Rohé* calculated that, whilst 5 lb beef — containing 1 lb protein — supplies ten days' protein requirements for the average adult, the production of that amount of beef absorbs (in corn and soya-bean feedstock) three *months'* supply of an adult's protein needs. In *Diet for a Small Planet*, Frances Moore Lappe† estimated that grains can produce five times more protein per acre than livestock, beans ten times and leafy vegetables fifteen times more. Into the bargain, it has been calculated‡ that the water expenditure in a vegan diet, taking into account crop irrigation and food preparation, is 300 gallons per person per day. The same figure for a person on a mixed meat diet, taking into account the water drunk by the livestock, used during its slaughter and during the preparation of the meat for the pot, is 2500 gallons. All these figures show very clearly that animal farming is a grossly inefficient way to use our natural resources and a completely inadequate answer to the needs of a planet on which many people are very short of food. Of course, much more could be said on this subject.

The Vegan Diet and Nutrition

The body needs protein, carbohydrates, vitamins, minerals and fats in the right combinations at the right times to function at an optimal level. The vegan diet can successfully provide all these components in

---

* Fred Rohé, *The Complete Book of Natural Foods*, Shambhala, 1983.
† Frances Moore Lappe, *Diet for a Small Planet*, Ballantine Books, New York, 1971.
‡ See Roshi Philip Kapleau, *A Buddhist Case for Vegetarianism*.

a natural and balanced manner as long as care is taken to ensure that the foods eaten are fresh and/or unrefined and that a good mixture of different foods is eaten every day. A mixed diet of whole grains and flours, pulses (including bean sprouts), nuts, seeds, vegetables (raw and very lightly cooked) and fresh fruit provides low-fat wholesome nutrients not denatured by overcooking and uncontaminated with the additives and saturated fats present in many refined foods, meats and dairy produce.

All our nutrients are best received as part of whole foods which also contain other natural substances that facilitate the assimilation of the nutrients by the body. This is a point more important to the vegan diet than any other since, although a good vegan diet is better than a mixed meat diet, a poor one is as bad, if not worse, than a poor mixed diet. Below is a short discussion on each of the main nutrient groups with reference to the vegan diet.

Protein

The question that most often bothers people about the vegan diet is whether it will provide enough protein. The question has been answered in the affirmative, both academically* and practically by the active and varied lives of many practising vegans and peoples who, because of where they live in the world and/or cultural tradition, follow a vegan diet naturally. The vegan foods – grains, pulses, nuts, seeds, vegetables (particularly green and raw ones) – and their derivatives such as plant milks and nut and seed spreads all contain protein. Eaten in combinations these foods provide protein of excellent quality.

The principle by which the protein quality of two or more foods eaten together is higher than the sum total of their individual parts is called 'complementarity'. This is explained in the following quote from *Protein-Rich Vegetarian Cookery* by David Scott †:

The proteins the body needs are composed of twenty-two amino acids. Eight of these acids, called the essential amino acids (EAA) cannot be synthesized by the body and must be supplied in the food we eat. All eight EAA are required simultaneously and each must be in the correct proportion to the others if the body is to use them efficiently. Fortunately for us, food proteins normally contain all eight EAAs, although one or more may be present in a disproportionately small amount. This small amount of one amino acid limits the usable amount of the remaining essential amino acids, since the body must be provided with them all at the same time in exactly the correct

---

* See, amongst many publications from the Vegan Society, *Plant Foods for Human Nutrition* by Dr J.W.T. Dickerson.
† David Scott, *Protein-Rich Vegetarian Cookery*, Rider, 1991.

profile. The EAA in short supply is called the limiting EAA and it affects the biological value (the percentage of protein present that can be utilized) of a particular foodstuff. Fortunately the amino acid in short supply in one food is often available in excess in another and vice-versa. By combining two or more complementary foods in one meal we obtain protein of much higher quality or biological value than the sum total obtained from eating the foods separately. For instance, most grains (e.g. rice, wheat, corn) or grain products are high in the amino acid tryptophan but low in lysine, while most pulses (e.g. beans, peas, lentils) are high in lysine and low in tryptophan. Thus a dish containing, say, rice and lentils would supply protein of higher biological value than the same total weight of just rice or just lentils.

The basic food groups contained in the vegan diet provide good complementary protein combinations and a mixed vegan diet will contain high-quality protein in sufficient quantity for most human requirements.

To ensure a good protein balance the source of the protein should be about 60 per cent grains, 35 per cent pulses and/or nuts and seeds and 5 per cent leafy green vegetables. These figures do not include nutrient requirements other than protein and for these the diet must also include vegetables (especially in salads) and fruit.

Fats

Fats provide a concentrated energy source and they contain the essential fat-soluble vitamins A, D and E. Every fat or oil contains active (unsaturated) or inactive (saturated) acids. The active acids are called essential fatty acids (EFA) and are contained in polyunsaturated fats. These fats essential to good nutrition are found in highest concentrations in vegetable oils. Saturated fats, which are linked to the risks of heart disease, high blood pressure and some cancers, occur in highest concentrations in animal fats including dairy products. The authors suggest that the intake of fats of any kind should be moderate but that vegetable oils such as corn, olive, peanut, safflower, sesame, sunflower and walnut should be used where possible. Incidentally, cold-pressed oils and margarines contain more natural nutrients than heat-extracted oils. Finally, the best way to eat fats is in the state in which they occur naturally, i.e., as part of the structure of nuts, seeds whole grains and beans.

Carbohydrates

Carbohydrates are the body's main source of energy. They are present in foods as starches and sugars and they are best obtained from foods not in a refined form but in combination with other essential nutrients. Such foods as whole-grain cereals and flour products (brown bread, brown pasta, etc.), pulses, vegetables (especially root vegetables) and fruit are good carbohydrate sources. Carbohydrates obtained from refined foods like sugar (and sugar-rich foods), white flour and saturated fats and oils, none of which contain many other nutrients, displace from the diet, by spoiling the appetite, other foods containing needed nutrients. Thus if we eat too much refined food we either go without nutrients we require or we have to eat more food than we need, starch wise, to get them; thus we get fat. A proper mixed vegan diet will supply all the carbohydrates needed and it won't leave that craving for more food that is often the result of eating refined foods.

Minerals and vitamins

The body cannot synthesize the vitamins and minerals it requires to function efficiently; they must therefore be supplied in the food we eat. A balanced mixed diet of whole grains, beans, lots of fresh raw vegetables and fruit, and some nuts and seeds, will ensure that the body is not deficient in vitamins or minerals with the possible exception of vitamin B12. This vitamin has been the cause of much of the controversy about the vegan diet since B12 occurs in flesh foods and dairy produce. Animals can synthesize B12 but it seems that human beings lose this facility unless they have been vegans all their lives.

There is, however, no evidence that vitamin B12 deficiency is more frequent in even the strictest vegan than in the carnivore*. It should be said that this may be because a person on a vegan diet is likely to be more careful about his or her diet than the average individual. The point is that anyone who is careless with their diet could suffer from a vitamin or mineral difficiency. Non-animal sources of vitamin B12 are miso (a fermented soya-bean paste), brewers' yeast (available in tablet form), sea kelp and some commercially available vegan foods, such as Barmene and Tastex (both yeast extracts) and soya milk (e.g. Plamil).

In a strict vegan diet it is advisable to include one of these sources in the diet. Incidentally, draught beer from the cask contains B12. Two pints is equal to the daily need for B12!

Raw vegetable salads

Raw vegetable salads are an important daily meal in the vegan diet. Food that is cooked is denatured and its quality reduced, depending on the length of time of the cooking process. Raw vegetables provide a

* *Mind and Body Encyclopaedia* (Orbis Publishing, 1971), ch. on vegetarianism; *The Lancet*, ii, p. 309, 1964.

large yield of vitamins and minerals, fibre and carbohydrate; green vegetables, in particular, contain high-quality protein. Raw salads are filling and, into the bargain, fat free. The best vegetables are grown in rich organic soil and, if you have a garden, this is the best place to obtain them. The next best choice is vegetables from a local grower or greengrocer and, finally, buy from the supermarket. Seasonal vegetables are likely to be in the choicest condition since they will not have travelled in refrigerated trucks or stood for days on the dockside awaiting collection.

Refined food

Much has been written about the harmful effects of eating too many refined foods and it can now be said quite firmly that a diet composed mainly of refined foods is too full of sugar, saturated fats, salt and additives and too short of fibre and naturally occurring nutrients to be good for your health. It is worth reiterating that the best foods to eat are those which are combined in the way nature intended. We should get our nutrients as part of a whole food and not as isolated fractions added to refined foods or made up into pills.

Changing to a Vegan Diet

This book is not advocating a change to a pure vegetarian diet, but offering it as an alternative. If, however, you wish to change your diet from one that contains a lot of meat and fish to a pure vegetarian one, it is sensible to do so slowly. Initially, cut red meats out of your diet and restrict your flesh-eating to poultry and fish. Slowly reduce your intake of white meats and fish and simultaneously increase the intake of dairy produce as well as whole grains, pulses, vegetables, fruits, nuts and seeds. This is a lacto-vegetarian diet and your body will not find it very different to your previous regime. Now start to increase your intake of non-dairy foods, particularly fresh and raw vegetables and fruit. At the same time reduce consumption of dairy produce. Do not eat refined foods and snacks, sugar-rich cakes, etc. Over the course of a year, if you are careful and increasingly aware about the foods you are eating, you will arrive at a balanced diet that suits your needs. This diet may be pure vegan or it may contain small amounts of cheese, milk or eggs; this will depend on your personal situation, requirements and feelings. The important thing is that you feel good about the food you eat, both physically and in relationship to other sentient beings and the life of the planet.

If you wish to start including more vegan dishes into your diet, we hope the following recipes will inspire you. As any practising vegan will tell you, the variety of vegan meals always astounds the unsuspecting carnivore who comes to dinner and expects nut cutlets and two veg.

Note: In the recipes given here specifically vegan ingredients such as soya milk, vegan 'cheese' or carob may be substituted by regular milk, cheese and chocolate if you wish.

Popular Vegan Protein Foods

Grains

Barley (whole)
Buckwheat and buckwheat flour
Corn and cornmeal
Millet
Rice (brown)
Rolled oats and oatmeal
Rye and rye flour
Wholewheat, wholemeal flour, bulgar (cracked wheat), couscous, wheatgerm and bran

Pulses

Aduki beans
Blackeye beans
Chick peas (garbanzos)
Kidney beans (including red beans and haricot beans)
Lentils
Peas
Soya beans, soya flour, tofu and miso

Nuts

Almonds
Brazils
Cashews
Hazels
Peanuts (classified as a pulse)
Pine nuts (pignolias)
Walnuts

Seeds

Sesame
Sunflower
Pumpkin

Vegetables

Dark leafy greens, e.g. spinach, broccoli, kale, etc.

Note: Lacto-vegetarian protein sources are as the above plus milk, cheese and eggs.

Soups, Starters and Dips

Vegetable soups, bean soups, grain soups or soups made from a combination of vegetables, beans and grains are the easiest dishes to serve to non-vegans since they are foods with which they are familiar. Soups are also very versatile in using up odd assortments of ingredients. Here we have given some standard and some unusual soup recipes but we hope each of them will give you ideas for your own improvisations since they all contain one or two unexpected combinations of ingredients.

The starters and dips are designed to grace a gourmet meal as well as to be everyday menu possibilities. The pâtés and dips, in particular, also make good light meals when served with a salad and bread.

Soups

Carrot and Oatmeal Soup   Serves 4–6

2 tablespoons (30 ml) vegetable oil
1 large onion, chopped
1 small clove garlic, crushed
2 teaspoons chopped fresh
  rosemary or 1 teaspoon dried
  rosemary

1 lb (450g) carrots, scrubbed and
  chopped
½ teaspoon curry powder
2 pints (1.1 litres) water
1 level tablespoon medium oatmeal
sea salt to taste

Heat the oil in a saucepan and sauté the onion, garlic and rosemary for 5 minutes. Add the carrots and curry powder, cover with the water, stir well and bring to the boil. Add the oatmeal and cook, covered, over a moderate heat, stirring occasionally until the carrots are soft (about 15 minutes). Liquidize the soup in a blender, add salt to taste, reheat and serve. Add more boiling water to the blender for a thinner soup.

Cream of Parsnip Soup   *Serves 6*

This is a good soup with which to start Christmas dinner.

2 tablespoons (30 ml) vegetable oil
1 large onion, chopped
1 clove garlic, crushed
1 bay leaf
2 teaspoons chopped fresh
rosemary *or* 1 teaspoon dried
rosemary
1 lb (450g) parsnips, scrubbed and
chopped

8 oz (225g) potatoes, scrubbed and
chopped
1¾ pints (1 litre) water
sea salt to taste
1 tablespoon chopped chives to
garnish (optional)

Heat the oil in a saucepan and sauté the onions, garlic, bay leaf and
rosemary for 5 minutes. Add the parsnips, potatoes and water. Stir
well, bring to the boil and simmer, covered, for 20 minutes. Remove
the bay leaf and liquidize the soup in a blender. Add salt to taste and
serve sprinkled with chopped chives.

Chilled Beetroot (Borscht) Soup   *Serves 4–6*

Try this soup on a really hot day; it is very refreshing as a starter or on
its own. Serve it as a sauce, too.

1 tablespoon (15 ml) vegetable oil
1 large onion, chopped
1 oz (25g) wholemeal flour
2 large raw beetroots, chopped
2–3 sticks celery
2 teaspoons chopped fresh mixed
herbs *or* 1 teaspoon dried mixed
herbs

8 oz (225g) tomatoes, chopped
1¾ pints (1 litre) water
1 clove garlic
soya sauce to taste
2 tablespoons chopped fresh
parsley
soya milk to garnish

Heat the oil in a pan and sauté the onion for 5 minutes. Add the flour
and stir it in well. Add the beetroot, celery, mixed herbs, tomatoes
and water. Stir well and bring to the boil. Reduce heat, cover and
simmer for 45 minutes (or 20 minutes in a pressure cooker). Liquidize
the contents of the pan in a blender with the garlic, soya sauce and
parsley. Pour the soup into a serving bowl and chill for at least 5 hours
in the fridge. Serve with a swirl of soya milk in each bowl.

Curried Leek and Potato Soup   *Serves 4–6*

This soup is a traditional winter warmer. As a variation, substitute lentils for some of the potato. For a complete meal serve the soup with hot herb bread (see pp. 76–7).

2 tablespoons (30 ml) vegetable oil
1 large onion, chopped
4 large leeks, cut in half, washed and sliced
12 oz (350g) potatoes, scrubbed and diced
1 pinch Aramé seaweed

2 teaspoons chopped fresh rosemary *or* 1 teaspoon dried rosemary
½ teaspoon curry powder
1¾ pints (1 litre) water
1 clove garlic
soya sauce to taste

Heat the oil in a saucepan or pressure cooker and sauté the onion and leeks for 5 minutes. Add the potatoes, seaweed, rosemary, curry powder and water. Stir well, bring to the boil, reduce heat, cover and cook for 20 minutes (7 minutes in a pressure cooker). Liquidize the soup in a blender with the garlic and soya sauce. Reheat and serve.

Mushroom and Barley Miso Soup   *Serves 4–6*

This is a lovely soup and is also good for people recovering from illness or an upset stomach. The soup is nutritious, easy to digest and the miso in it will help settle the system.

3 tablespoons (45 ml) vegetable oil
1 large onion, chopped
2 teaspoons chopped fresh thyme *or* 1 teaspoon dried thyme
12 oz (350g) mushrooms, chopped
1 level tablespoon pot barley, washed

1½ pints (0.8 litre) water
1 teaspoon miso
1 small clove garlic, crushed
1 teaspoon sea salt
soya sauce to taste
finely chopped fresh parsley to garnish

Heat the oil in a saucepan or pressure cooker and sauté the onions and thyme. After 5 minutes add the mushrooms and cook for a further 2 minutes. Add the pot barley and the water. Bring to the boil, reduce heat, cover and cook for 1–1½ hours or 30 minutes under pressure. Liquidize ¼ pint (150 ml) of the soup in a blender with the miso, garlic, salt and soya sauce. Pour the blended soup back into the saucepan, mix well, reheat and serve with lots of chopped parsley to garnish.

'MAJESTIC'.   'KING EDWARD'.   'DR. McINTOSH'.

Rich Tomato and Rice Soup   *Serves 4–6*

This is a flavoursome 'sweet sour' soup that is filling and nutritious.

2 tablespoons (30 ml) vegetable oil
1 large onion, chopped
1 teaspoon dried basil
1 bay leaf
1 tablespoon wholemeal flour
1 small carrot, scrubbed and
  chopped
1 stick celery, chopped
1 teaspoon honey *or* brown sugar
1 tablespoon (15 ml) cider vinegar
14 oz (400g) canned tomatoes,
  chopped (reserve juice)

1 pint (0·5 litre) water
1 small clove garlic, crushed
soya sauce to taste
sea salt to taste
2 fl oz (50 ml) soya milk
3 tablespoons cooked rice
2 tablespoons roasted sunflower
  seeds to garnish (see p. 63 for
  roasting method)

Heat the oil in a pan and sauté the onion, basil and bay leaf for 5 minutes. Stir in the flour. Add the carrot, celery, honey or sugar, cider vinegar, tomatoes with their juice and the water. Bring to the boil, reduce heat, cover and cook for 20 minutes. Liquidize the soup in a blender with the garlic, soya sauce and salt. Add the soya milk and cooked rice. Reheat and serve with a sprinkling of roasted sunflower seeds.

Spring Nettle Soup   *Serves 4–6*

Nettles are a perennial plant that can be cooked just like spinach. They are particularly good in the spring when the leaves are young and tender. Use the tops of the plants for the mildest flavour.

2 tablespoons (30 ml) vegetable oil
1 medium onion, chopped
1 small clove garlic, crushed
1 large potato, scrubbed and
  chopped

1 lb (450g) young nettles
1¾ pints (1 litre) water
1 teaspoon (5 ml) lemon juice
½ teaspoon ground nutmeg
sea salt to taste

Heat the oil in a pan and sauté the onion and garlic for 5 minutes. Add the potato, nettles, water and lemon juice. Bring to the boil, reduce heat, cover and cook for 20 minutes. Liquidize the soup in a blender with the nutmeg and salt. Reheat and serve.

Watercress and Potato Soup   *Serves 4–6*

The peppery taste of the watercress gives the soup a 'spiky' flavour and
a warming quality that is much appreciated on a cold day.

2 tablespoons (30 ml) vegetable oil
1 large onion, chopped
1 small clove garlic, crushed
2 teaspoons chopped fresh
   marjoram *or* 1 teaspoon dried
   marjoram

1 lb (450g) potatoes, scrubbed and
   chopped
1¾ pints (1 litre) water
1 bunch watercress, discard
   yellowed leaves
soya sauce to taste

Heat the oil in a pan and sauté the onion, garlic and marjoram for 5
minutes. Add the potatoes and water, bring to the boil, reduce heat,
cover and cook for 20 minutes. Liquidize the contents of the pan in a
blender with the watercress and soya sauce. Reheat and serve.

Spiced Yellow Split Pea Soup   *Serves 4–6*

This is simple to prepare and cook but is very tasty. Served with bread
it makes a good light meal.

4 oz (100g) split peas, soaked
1¾ pints (1 litre) water
1 bay leaf
1 large carrot, scrubbed and cut
   into large chunks
1 medium potato, scrubbed and
   quartered

1 large onion, quartered
½ teaspoon ground cumin
½ teaspoon ground coriander
½ teaspoon garam masala
2 tablespoons (30 ml) soya sauce
salt to taste
1 tablespoon vegetable margarine

Put all the ingredients, except the margarine, into the pot or pressure
cooker. Bring to the boil, reduce heat, cover and cook for 45 minutes
(20 minutes in a pressure cooker). Liquidize the soup with the
margarine in a blender. Reheat and serve.

Cream of Artichoke Soup   *Serves 4–6*

Jerusalem artichokes are an underrated vegetable and you should try them when available. They take a little longer to clean than potatoes but are worth the extra effort.

2 tablespoons (30 ml) vegetable oil
2 medium onions, chopped
1 teaspoon chopped fresh rosemary
  or ½ teaspoon dried rosemary
1½ lb (700g) Jerusalem artichokes,
  scrubbed and knobs removed

1¾ pints (1 litre) water
1 tablespoon medium oatmeal
1 small clove garlic, crushed
2 tablespoons (30 ml) soya sauce
sea salt to taste

Heat the oil in a pan and sauté the onions and rosemary for 5 minutes. Add the artichokes, water and oatmeal. Bring to the boil, reduce heat, cover and simmer for 30 minutes (15 minutes under pressure). Liquidize the contents of the pan in a blender with the garlic, soya sauce and salt. Reheat and serve.

Minestrone Soup   *Serves 6*

This is an excellent variation on the celebrated Italian soup. It is versatile and can be served as a starter or with bread as a light meal.

2 tablespoons (30 ml) vegetable oil
3 medium onions, chopped
1 large clove garlic, crushed
1 bay leaf
1 large carrot, scrubbed and diced
  into ¼ in (5 mm) cubes
2 sticks celery, finely chopped
1 large potato, scrubbed and cut
  into ¼ in (5 mm) cubes

14 oz (400g) canned tomatoes,
  finely chopped
½ teaspoon curry powder
1½ pints (0·8 litre) water
2 oz (50g) wholemeal macaroni
soya sauce to taste
2 tablespoons grated vegan cheese
  to garnish

Heat the oil in a pan and sauté the onions, garlic and bay leaf for 5 minutes. Add the carrot, celery, potato, tomatoes, curry powder and water. Bring to the boil, reduce heat, cover and cook for 20 minutes. Add the macaroni, stir well and cook for a further 12 minutes. Flavour the soup with soya sauce and serve with a sprinkling of vegan cheese.

Thick Butterbean Soup   *Serves 6*

The butterbeans give the soup a creamy flavour but this is also a good recipe to use with other beans such as haricot or chick peas.

2 tablespoons (30 ml) vegetable oil
1 large onion, chopped
1 bay leaf
1 clove garlic, crushed
1 teaspoon dried mixed herbs
1 medium potato, scrubbed and chopped
2 medium carrots, scrubbed and chopped

2 sticks celery, scrubbed and chopped
½ teaspoon kelp powder
1¾ pints (1 litre) water
6 oz (175g) butterbeans, pre-soaked and cooked tender
sea salt to taste

Heat the oil in a pan and sauté the onion, bay leaf, garlic and herbs for 5 minutes. Add the potato, carrots, celery, kelp powder and water. Stir well and bring to the boil, reduce heat, cover and cook for 15–20 minutes or until the vegetables are tender. Remove the bay leaf, liquidize the vegetables and liquid with half the butterbeans. Salt to taste. Combine the blended soup with the remaining butterbeans, reheat and serve.

Lentil and Tomato Soup   *Serves 4–6*

3 tablespoons (45 ml) vegetable oil
2 large onions, chopped
1 small clove garlic, crushed
2 teaspoons chopped fresh rosemary *or* 1 teaspoon dried rosemary
1¾ pints (1 litre) lentil cooking liquid and water
8 oz (225g) cooked lentils, drained (reserve cooking liquid)

1 large carrot, scrubbed and chopped
1 stick celery, scrubbed and chopped
14 oz (400g) canned tomatoes, chopped
1 large pinch Aramé seaweed
1 teaspoon miso
½ teaspoon ground cumin
sea salt to taste

Heat the oil in a pan and sauté the onions, garlic and rosemary for 5 minutes. Add the liquids and the lentils, carrot, celery, tomatoes and seaweed. Bring to the boil, reduce heat, cover and simmer for 20 minutes (7 minutes in a pressure cooker). Liquidize the contents of the pan with the miso, cumin and salt to taste. Reheat and serve.

Starters and Dips

Cashew Nut and Tofu Pâté   *Serves 6*

This vegan pâté needs almost no cooking and it is very useful if preparation time is limited. For special occasions use the wine as suggested. Serve with brown Melba toast.

1 tablespoon (15 ml) olive oil
1 small onion, diced
1 small clove garlic, crushed
4 oz (100g) cashew nuts, toasted
  and ground
6 oz (175g) tofu (beancurd),
  drained

4 tablespoons (60 ml) white wine
  or water
2 tablespoons chopped parsley
sea salt to taste

Heat the oil in a shallow pan and sauté the onion and garlic until softened (about 5 minutes). Add this mixture to the nuts in a mixing bowl, then mash in the tofu. Stir in the wine, parsley and salt. Press the pâté into individual ramekins, smooth the top of the mixture and serve.

Mushroom Pâté   *Serves 4*

This is a good pâté to serve to non-vegetarian guests. The colour and flavour of the mushrooms give the pâté a mild flavour reminiscent of a meat pâté.

2 tablespoons (30 ml) vegetable oil
1 large onion, peeled and chopped
2 teaspoons chopped fresh
  rosemary *or* 1 teaspoon dried
  rosemary
1 small clove garlic, crushed

12 oz (350g) mushrooms, washed
  and chopped
2 tablespoons wholemeal flour
1 tablespoon soya flour
1 teaspoon miso
soya sauce to taste

Heat the oil in a pan and sauté the onion, rosemary and garlic for about 5 minutes. Add the mushrooms and cook over a moderate heat for a further 5 minutes. Add the flour and soya flour and cook, stirring, for a further 10 minutes. Put the mixture into a blender and add the soya sauce and miso. Blend the mixture to a smooth paste and serve the pâté smoothed down in individual ramekins.

Butterbean and Olive Starter   *Serves 4*

This is a tasty, simple, colourful and healthy starter.

4 oz (100g) black olives, stoned
and chopped
2 oz (50g) carrots, scrubbed and
finely grated
4 oz (100g) butterbeans, soaked
and cooked, *or* 8 oz (225g)
tinned butterbeans, drained

2 teaspoons dried oregano
1 teaspoon (5 ml) white wine
1 oz (25g) roasted cashew nuts
chopped parsley to garnish

Mix the olives and carrot with the butterbeans. Stir in the oregano, wine and nuts. Serve cold garnished with parsley.

Stuffed Celery and Dates   *Serves 4*

Serve as a starter or snack or as part of a buffet meal.

a little tofu dressing (see p. 89)
4 oz (100g) hazelnuts, ground

4 sticks celery, cut into 2 in (5 cm)
lengths
12 fresh dates, halved and stoned

Mash a little tofu dressing into the hazelnuts and fill the celery chunks and date halves with the mixture. Arrange the stuffed celery and dates on a plate and serve.

Sharon's Fruit Delight   *Serves 4*

This starter and the one below are good dinner-party recipes when you haven't much time, especially if the rest of the meal is to be very filling.

1 persimmon, cut in half and flesh
scooped out
1 orange, peeled and chopped

1 pear, quartered and cored
orange juice to taste

Put all the ingredients into a blender. Blend until smooth, adding as much orange juice as necessary to get a medium-thick texture. Transfer the delight to individual dishes and chill before serving.

Tropical Fruit Refresher   *Serves 4*

½ paw paw, flesh scooped out
1 large banana, peeled
2 kiwi fruits, flesh scooped out

½ pint (275 ml) orange juice
4 thin slices of orange

Put all the ingredients except the orange slices into a blender and liquidize until smooth. Chill and serve in small glasses, each decorated with a slice of orange.

Soya Bean Dip with Olive and Lemon Garnish   *Serves 4–6*

This is a very nice dip but preparing the cooked soya beans is a long business and should be carried out in conjunction with cooking soya beans for at least one other dish. Alternatively, make this dip from other cooked or canned cooked beans, e.g. chick peas.

6 tablespoons (90 ml) olive oil
2 large onions, finely chopped
8 oz (225g) soya beans, soaked and cooked for 4 hours (*or* 2 hours under pressure) and drained
5 tablespoons (75 ml) lemon juice
1 teaspoon honey
sea salt to taste

Garnish
2 tablespoons (30 ml) olive oil
2 tablespoons (30 ml) lemon juice
3 tablespoons chopped parsley
1 teaspoon paprika

Heat the oil in a pan and sauté the onions until soft (about 5 minutes). Put the onions and oil in a blender with the beans, lemon juice, honey and salt. Liquidize until smooth. Transfer the dip to a serving bowl. Mix the garnish ingredients together and trickle the mixture over the dip. Serve.

Avocado Dip   *Serves 4*

This dip is a guaranteed children's favourite. It is also ideal for babies, but leave out the salt and onion. For a more adventurous dip see the Avocado and Lemon Dip, recipe overleaf.

2–3 small ripe avocados, peeled and cubed
1 teaspoon onion, finely chopped

2 teaspoons (10 ml) lemon juice
sea salt to taste

Mash the avocado with a fork. Add the other ingredients and mix well. Serve the dip with rice cakes or crackers and sticks of carrot, celery, fennel, green pepper or other crudités.

AVOCADO.   PUMPKIN.   FIG.

Avocado and Lemon Dip   *Serves 4–6*

The sweet flesh of the avocado perfectly partners the sour lemon juice.

2 medium-sized ripe avocados,
  flesh scooped out
juice and grated rind of 1 lemon
2 cloves garlic, crushed

salt and black pepper to taste
up to ¼ pint (150 ml) vegetable oil
  (olive oil is best)

Put the avocado flesh, lemon rind, lemon juice and garlic into a blender (or mix by hand) and make a smooth paste. Leaving the paste in the blender, add salt and black pepper to taste. Now put the blender on the slowest speed and slowly add the oil. Stop when the mixture no longer absorbs the oil easily or when the taste is to your liking.

Aubergine and Tahini Dip   *Serves 4–6*

This rich Middle Eastern-influenced dip is usually served with pitta bread. It is eaten as a starter or with a green salad as a light meal.

2 small aubergines
4 fl oz (100 ml) tahini
juice of 1 lemon
1 clove garlic, crushed

2 tablespoons finely chopped fresh
  parsley
salt to taste
black olives to garnish

Lightly oil the aubergines and place them in an oven, preheated to 350°F (180°C, gas mark 4), for about 1 hour or until the aubergine interiors are well cooked. Rub or peel the skins off (the job is more easily done holding the aubergine under a cold tap). Combine the aubergine flesh with the remaining ingredients and either beat them into a smooth paste by hand or with a blender. Serve garnished with black olives.

Tahini and Lemon Dip   *Serves 4*

This is a straightforward, quite thin, tahini dip which is also good, hot, as a sauce with grains or vegetables.

4 fl oz (100 ml) tahini
1 clove garlic, crushed
2 fl oz (50 ml) water
juice of 1 lemon
1½ tablespoons (25 ml) vegetable
  oil (olive oil is best)

salt to taste
chopped parsley to garnish
pinch of cayenne to garnish

Blend or thoroughly mix the tahini, garlic, water, lemon juice and oil. Add more water if the dip is too thick. Add salt to taste. Serve garnished with parsley and a sprinkling of cayenne.

Chick Peas and Tahini Dip

This is a good way to use up leftover cooked chick peas (or red beans or haricot beans). The dip is quite filling but the mint and lemon give it a refreshing flavour.

8 oz (225g) cooked chick peas, drained
4 fl oz (100 ml) tahini
juice of 1 lemon

1 tablespoon chopped fresh mint *or* 1 teaspoon dried mint
salt and black pepper to taste
2 teaspoons grated lemon rind

Blend the chick peas, tahini and lemon juice together to form a smooth paste. Add the mint, salt and black pepper to taste. Transfer the dip to a serving bowl and garnish with lemon rind; chill and serve.

Vegetable Dishes

Regarding ingredients, vegetable dishes are no problem for the vegan cook. Apart from the recipes given here all the usual plain, vegetable-only dishes we are used to are fine for the vegan diet. If you can, find a supply of pesticide-free, organically grown vegetables. If you cannot, it would be worth asking your greengrocer or local whole-food store to start stocking them. (The more interest there is from the public, the sooner local farmers will take note!) Always wash vegetables thoroughly and, where appropriate, give them a good scrub. Cook the vegetables in the minimum of time and minimum of water necessary. They should retain their colour and crunch. Where possible, always use fresh vegetables. The tinned and frozen varieties invariably lose some of their quality (or life force) during the processing procedures. For the same reason do not peel vegetables unless absolutely necessary, as the skin contains many nutrients.

Savoury Potato Cakes _Serves 2–3_

These are good with a salad in the summer, with lightly boiled or steamed vegetables in colder months, or as a snack.

4 oz (100g) raw potato, grated	1 teaspoon dried sage
1 medium onion, grated	sea salt to taste
2 oz (50g) soya flour	oil for shallow frying

Combine all the ingredients together in a bowl and mix well. Form the mixture into 6–8 small, hamburger-shaped potato cakes. Heat the oil in a frying pan and fry the cakes for about 5 minutes, turning them once during this time. Serve immediately.

Vegan 'Cheese' and Potato Pie   *Serves 4*

We recommend this pie with Sweet-and-Sour Red Cabbage with Chestnuts (see p. 37) and a green salad.

2 large onions, sliced
2 tablespoons (30 ml) vegetable oil
3 bay leaves
2 teaspoons (10 ml) soya sauce
6 oz (175g) vegan 'cheese', grated (see p. 77)

12 oz (350g) potatoes, peeled, boiled and mashed
nutmeg to taste
2 medium tomatoes, sliced

Preheat oven to 400°F (200°C, gas mark 6). Sauté the onions in the oil with the bay leaves until they are transparent. Add the soya sauce and lay the mixture over the base of a suitably sized baking dish. Mix half the cheese with the mashed potato, add nutmeg to taste and spread the mixture over the onions. Top it all with the rest of the grated cheese and bake the pie for 20 minutes. Finally, top with slices of tomato and flash cook the pie under a hot grill or in the hot oven to finish.

Stuffed Aubergines   *Serves 4*

These stuffed aubergine boats are topped with roasted almonds. Serve with broccoli, spinach or other greens. For a substantial meal serve with rice, a tomato sauce and greens.

2 medium-sized aubergines
1 tablespoon (15 ml) vegetable oil
2 large onions, chopped
2 cloves garlic, crushed
6 oz (175g) mushrooms, chopped
4 large tomatoes, skinned and chopped
1 teaspoon miso paste

3 oz (75g) wholemeal breadcrumbs
1 oz (25g) wheatgerm
4 oz (100g) blanched almonds, chopped
1 tablespoon chopped parsley
1 teaspoon (5 ml) lemon juice
salt and black pepper to taste

Preheat oven to 350°F (180°C, gas mark 4). Prick the aubergines four or five times each with a fork to prevent the skins from bursting, place them on a lightly greased baking tray and bake for 30 minutes in the preheated oven, turning once. Leave the oven on. Cut the aubergines in halves lengthways and scoop out much of the flesh but leave solid walls. Chop the flesh. Heat the oil in a pan and fry the onions over a moderate heat for 3 minutes, stirring occasionally. Add the garlic and fry for 1 minute. Add the mushrooms to the pan with the tomatoes and miso. Simmer the mixture for 5 minutes and then add the aubergine flesh, breadcrumbs and wheatgerm, half the almonds, the parsley and the lemon juice. Season to taste with salt and black pepper and simmer for a further 2–3 minutes. Fill the aubergine shells with the mixture. Put them on the baking tray, top with the remaining almonds and bake in the hot oven for 20–25 minutes.

Vegetable Pasties   *Makes about 12 pasties*

The vegetables given here are only suggestions; use others more to your taste or more easily available if you wish. Serve on their own with salad, or with a cheese sauce poured over and accompanied by boiled grains.

1 large potato, scrubbed *or* peeled and diced
1 large carrot, scrubbed *or* peeled and diced
4 oz (100g) fresh peas *or* frozen peas, defrosted
4 oz (100g) French beans, topped, tailed, stringed and chopped

1 lb (450g) wholemeal shortcrust pastry (see p. 96)
½ teaspoon miso
1 fl oz (25 ml) boiling water
¼ teaspoon kelp powder
2 tablespoons chopped parsley
2 fl oz (50 ml) soya milk

Put the potato and carrot into a pan and barely cover with water. Bring to the boil and cook for 6–8 minutes. Add the peas and beans and simmer until all the vegetables are tender. Drain, rinse the cooked vegetables under cold water and set aside. Preheat oven to 350°F (180°C, gas mark 4). Roll out the pastry thinly (about ¼ in (5 mm)) and cut into 6 in (15 cm) rounds. Dissolve the miso in boiling water, add the cooked vegetables, kelp and parsley and mix well together. Put a dessertspoonful of this mixture on the centre of each pastry round. Fold the rounds into half-moon shapes and press the edges together, using water to help them stick if necessary. Brush the top of each half-moon with soya milk, put the pasties on a lightly greased baking tray and bake in the preheated oven for 15 minutes.

Courgette and Tomato Pie   *Serves 4*

This pie is good at any time but is especially economical and tasty in the summer when tomatoes and courgettes are plentiful and cheap and fresh basil is available.

6 oz (175g) wholemeal shortcrust pastry (see p. 96)
4 oz (100g) onion, sliced
2 cloves garlic, crushed
1 tablespoon (15 ml) olive oil
1 lb (450g) fresh tomatoes, skinned and chopped

1 lb (450g) courgettes, sliced
2 teaspoons freshly chopped basil *or* 1 teaspoon dried basil
sea salt to taste
1 teaspoon arrowroot

Preheat oven to 400°F (200°C, gas mark 6). Roll out half the pastry and line a pie dish with it. Sauté the onion and garlic in the oil in a pan for about 5 minutes. Add the tomatoes, courgettes and basil. Bring the mixture to the boil, cover, reduce heat and simmer for 5 minutes. At the end of the cooking time add salt to taste and thicken the mixture with the arrowroot pre-blended with a little cold water. Pour the mixture into the pastry case. Roll out the remaining pastry for the top, put the top into place and seal the edges with the tines of a fork. Bake for 25–30 minutes in the preheated oven.

Tomato Oatcakes   *Makes 4 oatcakes*

These are delicious with home-made apple chutney (see p. 89).

¼ pint (150 ml) tomato sauce (see p. 72), liquidized
2 oz (50g) porridge oats
1 teaspoon yeast extract
1 teaspoon paprika

3–4 tablespoons wholemeal flour
salt to taste
corn oil or other vegetable oil to shallow fry

Mix together the tomato sauce, oats, yeast extract and paprika. Add just enough flour to make the mixture bind together well. Form the mixture into 4 round oatcakes about ¼ in (5 mm) thick and coat them in flour seasoned with salt to taste. Heat a little oil in a frying pan and fry the oatcakes on both sides until golden brown (about 2½ minutes each side).

Mushroom and Rice Stuffed Marrow   *Serves 4*

The stuffing used in this recipe is also good for stuffing other vegetables such as peppers, aubergines, courgettes, etc.

1 tablespoon (15 ml) vegetable oil
1 medium onion, chopped
1 clove garlic, crushed
4 oz (100g) mushrooms, chopped
2 oz (50g) cashew nuts, finely
  chopped
8 oz (225g) cooked brown rice

1 teaspoon yeast extract
1 tablespoon chopped parsley
2 teaspoons chopped fresh thyme
  or 1 teaspoon dried thyme
1 marrow (large enough for 4
  people), sliced lengthwise and
  seeds removed

Preheat oven to 400°F (200°C, gas mark 6). Heat the oil in a frying pan and sauté the onion and garlic for about 5 minutes. Remove the pan from the heat and add the mushrooms, nuts, rice, yeast extract, parsley and thyme. Mix well. Fill one half of the marrow with the mixture and place the other half on top. Place the stuffed marrow in a lightly greased casserole dish and bake in the preheated oven for 1 hour.

Brazil Nut and Rice Stuffed Green Peppers   *Serves 4*

If Brazil nuts are unavailable use walnuts or almonds.

4 medium green peppers
1 medium onion, chopped
1 tablespoon (15 ml) vegetable oil
1 small red pepper, seeded, cored
  and finely chopped

1 teaspoon miso
8 oz (225g) cooked brown rice
4 oz (100g) Brazil nuts, chopped
sea salt to taste

Preheat oven to 350°F (180°C, gas mark 4). Plunge the green peppers into a pan of boiling water for 2 minutes. Then cut the tops off them (reserve these), scoop out the seeds and cores and discard. Sauté the onion in the vegetable oil in a saucepan for 5 minutes. Add the red pepper and cook for a further 2 minutes. Dissolve the miso in the hot juices in the pan. Stir in the rice and nuts, mix well and add salt to taste. Stuff the peppers with this mixture. Place the stuffed peppers on a lightly greased baking tray. Put the lids back on and bake for 30 minutes in the preheated oven.

CELERIAC.

CARROT ~ DIFFERENT ROOT VARIETIES.

Aubergine and Potato Curry

Serves 4

Serve with rice and/or chapattis and chutney.

2 tablespoons (30 ml) vegetable oil
1 large clove garlic, crushed
½ teaspoon ground ginger
½ teaspoon ground turmeric
½ teaspoon cumin seeds
½ teaspoon mustard seed
1 pinch each of cayenne, ground coriander and cinnamon
1 large aubergine, diced in large cubes, salted for ½ hour, rinsed

1 large green pepper, seeded, cored, and cut in large strips
2 large potatoes, scrubbed and cubed
½ pint (275 ml) water
4 tomatoes, quartered
½ oz (15g) vegetable margarine

Heat the oil and sauté the garlic and spices for 5 minutes. Having rinsed the excess juice out of the diced aubergine, add the pieces to the mixture. Cook for 2 minutes, then add the green pepper and potatoes with the water. Bring to the boil, cover, reduce heat and simmer for 30 minutes. Add the tomatoes and margarine. Cook for 2 more minutes and serve.

Sweet-and-Sour Red Cabbage with Chestnuts

Serves 4

This dish is good on its own with cooked grains and is also ideal for spicing up a bland savoury dish.

1 medium onion, chopped
1 tablespoon (15 ml) vegetable oil
½ medium cooking apple, chopped
1 small red cabbage, thinly sliced
1 oz (25g) sultanas
2 teaspoons (10 ml) lemon juice
1 tablespoon brown sugar
2 teaspoons (10 ml) soya sauce

1 teaspoon (5 ml) cider vinegar
½ pint (275 ml) water
2 oz (50g) dried chestnuts, covered with water and soaked overnight, then cooked in their soaking water for 1 hour
1 teaspoon arrowroot mixed with 1 tablespoon (15 ml) water

Sauté the onion in the oil in a pan for 5 minutes. Add the apple and cook for 1 minute. Add the red cabbage, sultanas, lemon juice, brown sugar, soya sauce and cider vinegar. Stir well and pour in the water. Bring to the boil, cover, reduce heat and simmer for about 15 minutes. Stir in the chestnuts and thicken with the arrowroot. Cook and stir for another few minutes and serve.

Jerusalem Artichokes, Greens and Garlic   *Serves 4*

Use Jerusalem artichokes in season; they are a lovely vegetable and a nice change from potatoes.

3 cloves garlic, crushed
2 tablespoons (30 ml) vegetable oil
8 oz (225g) Jerusalem artichokes,
  scrubbed, knobs cut off, sliced

4 oz (100g) greens (broccoli, kale,
  spinach, etc.) or sprout tops,
  chopped
soya sauce to taste

Sauté the garlic in the vegetable oil in a pan for 1 minute. Add the Jerusalem artichokes and cook with stirring for about 7 minutes over a moderate heat, adding a little water if necessary to prevent browning. Add the greens and cook for a further 5 minutes. Season to taste with soya sauce and serve immediately.

Jerusalem Artichokes in Tomato Sauce   *Serves 4*

8 oz (225g) Jerusalem artichokes,
  scrubbed and knobs cut off

½ pint (275 ml) tomato sauce (see
  p. 72)

Preheat oven to 375°F (190°C, gas mark 5). Put the Jerusalem artichokes, whole, in a greased casserole dish. Pour the tomato sauce over them. Cover and bake in the preheated oven for 45 minutes or until the artichokes are tender.

Spicy Beetroot and Tomato Dish   *Serves 6*

When liquidized this dish makes a colourful sauce for savoury meals or rissoles.

2 large onions, chopped
3 cloves garlic, crushed
2 teaspoons ground cumin
2 tablespoons (30 ml) vegetable oil
1 lb (450g) raw beetroot, scrubbed
  and diced

14 oz (400g) tinned tomatoes,
  chopped
sea salt to taste

Preheat oven to 350°F (180°C, gas mark 4). Sauté the onions, garlic and cumin for 5 minutes in the vegetable oil, in an ovenproof dish or casserole dish. Add the beetroot, stir, pour in the tomatoes and season to taste with salt. Bring to the boil, cover and bake for 1 hour in the preheated oven.

Roast Parsnips

Serves 4 as a side dish

1 lb (450g) parsnips, scrubbed and   vegetable oil for roasting
  sliced lengthwise

Preheat oven to 425°F (220°C, gas mark 7). Boil the parsnips for 10
minutes in salted water to just cover. Strain and dry them in a pan over
low heat while heating the oil ¼ in (5 mm) deep in a baking tin in the
oven. Put the parsnips in the hot oil and turn them around to cover all
sides with oil. Return baking tin to the oven and bake until the
parnships are brown and tender, about 45 minutes. Turn them
occasionally during this time.

Winter Vegetable Hot Pot

Serves 6

This is a warm and filling winter dish.

1 lb (450g) potatoes, scrubbed and   8 oz (225g) tomatoes, scalded and
  thickly sliced   skinned
1 small turnip, scrubbed and thinly   1 tablespoon miso
  sliced   ½ teaspoon kelp powder
2 medium carrots, scrubbed and   ¼ teaspoon curry powder
  thinly sliced   1 pint (0·5 litre) boiling vegetable
4 oz (100g) mushrooms, left whole   stock *or* water
1 large onion, sliced

Preheat oven to 350°F (180°C, gas mark 4). Place all the vegetables in a
casserole dish in alternate layers. Stir the miso, kelp and curry powder
into the boiling stock or water and pour this over the vegetables.
Cover and bake for 1½ hours in the preheated oven.

turnip

Braised Celery and Carrots   *Serves 4 as a side dish*

Serve this as a side dish to a main course or on its own with cooked grains and a salad.

2 large onions, sliced
1 tablespoon (15 ml) vegetable oil
4 carrots, cut into thin strips
6 large sticks celery, split in two
  lengthwise and cut in half

1 pint (0·5 litre) vegetable stock *or*
  water with 2 teaspoons Vecon
sea salt to taste

Preheat oven to 325°F (170°C, gas mark 3). Sauté the onions in the oil in an ovenproof saucepan or casserole dish for 5 minutes. Place the carrots on top of the onions and lay the celery over the mixture. Cover the vegetables with the stock and season with salt. Cover the pan or dish and cook in the preheated oven for about 1 hour or until the vegetables are tender. Baste the vegetables every now and then with the cooking liquid.

Aubergine and Tomato Bake   *Serves 4*

This is a quick and simple dish to prepare. Serve it with crusty bread and a salad.

3 aubergines, thinly sliced, salted
  for ½ hour, rinsed
3 medium onions, sliced
6 medium tomatoes, sliced

3 tablespoons (45 ml) natural
  tomato ketchup (e.g. the Whole
  Earth brand)
1 teaspoon honey
sea salt to taste

Preheat oven to 350°F (180°C, gas mark 4). Rinse off the excess moisture in the aubergines and put them into a lightly greased casserole dish with the onions, tomatoes, ketchup, honey and salt. Cover and bake for 1 hour.

Mushroom, Onion and Tomato Crumble   *Serves 2*

1 large onion, sliced in rings
2 tablespoons (30 ml) vegetable oil
8 oz (225g) mushrooms, washed
  and halved
3 tomatoes, scalded, peeled and
  chopped

1 teaspoon yeast extract
2 oz (50g) wholemeal breadcrumbs
1 oz (25g) vegetable margarine

Preheat oven to 400°F (200°C, gas mark 6). Sauté the onion in the vegetable oil in an ovenproof pan or casserole dish for 5 minutes.

Layer the mushrooms and tomatoes over the onion. Spread the yeast extract as evenly as possible over the vegetables and then sprinkle the breadcrumbs to make the crumble. Dot with margarine, cover and bake for 20 minutes, removing the cover 5 minutes before the end of the cooking time.

Vegetable Crumble

Serves 4–6

This is a rich, rosemary-flavoured vegetable dish guaranteed to satisfy the gourmet and the hungry. Serve the dish with carrot or beetroot soup (see pp. 17 and 18), as a sauce, to add colour and flavour.

2 onions, chopped
2 teaspoons chopped fresh rosemary *or* 1 teaspoon dried rosemary
2 tablespoons (30 ml) vegetable oil
2 carrots, scrubbed, cut into large chunks
2 sticks celery, coarsely chopped
1 large potato, peeled, cut in large chunks
1 medium parsnip, peeled, cut in large chunks
1 small turnip, peeled, cut in large chunks

1 small swede, peeled, cut in large chunks
8 oz (225g) mushrooms, chopped
8 oz (225g) tomatoes, peeled and chopped
¼ small cauliflower, cut in large florets
1 tablespoon miso
6 oz (175g) wholemeal flour
2 oz (50g) rolled oats
3 oz (75g) margarine
1 oz (25g) sunflower seeds
salt to taste

Preheat oven to 400°F (200°C, gas mark 6). Sauté the onions and rosemary in the oil in a large saucepan for 5 minutes. Add the rest of the vegetables, cover and cook for 15 minutes, adding a little water if necessary to prevent browning. At the end of this time use a little of the juice from the pan to dissolve the miso and stir it in. Remove the pan from the heat. Make the crumble by rubbing the margarine into the flour and oats until you have formed a crumble-like mixture. Add to this the sunflower seeds and salt to taste. Put the cooked vegetables into a casserole dish or tray and cover them with the crumble mix. Bake for 20 minutes or until nicely browned in the hot oven.

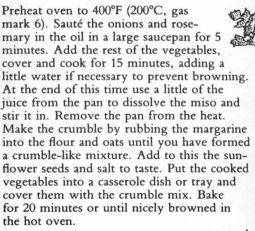

swede

Grain Recipes

Grains are embryonic plants. They are small packages of nourishment and energy and they provide the world with its principal food source. Grains contain protein and carbohydrate and many vitamins in excellent proportion for our particular nutritional needs. They are fine foods.

The main grains available in this country are brown rice, barley, buckwheat (sometimes called kasha; it is really a seed, not a grain, but is always classed with grains), bulgar wheat (made from wholewheat grains which are parboiled, dried and then cracked), millet, wholewheat grains (berries) and oats. If possible buy organically grown grains and always whole, unrefined grains, e.g. brown rice not white rice.

All the grains are very good cooked on their own in water and then served as a side dish to vegetables and/or a sauce, or combined with raw vegetables and made into a salad. Cooked grains can also be mixed with other ingredients and baked or used to stuff vegetables, make rissoles and so on. Some grains benefit from dry roasting before boiling in water and this is particularly the case with buckwheat (kasha) which loses some of its flavour if it is not dry roasted. The process is simple. Heat a pan over a medium to high flame, do not add any oil, pour in the grain concerned and stir it around in the pan with a wooden spoon until it starts to brown a little. Remove the pan from the heat. The grain is now ready for cooking.

To cook grains add one volume of grain to about 2–3 volumes of boiling, slightly salted water. Return the water to the boil, reduce heat, cover the pan with a close-fitting lid and gently simmer until all the water is absorbed and the grains are tender. You will have to experiment to discover the exact amount of water and cooking time per type of grain – but the following is a rough guide.

Grain (1 volume)	Water (volumes)	Cooking time
Barley	2½–3	1 hour
Brown rice	2	40 minutes
Buckwheat	2	15–20 minutes
Bulgar wheat	2	15–20 minutes
Millet	2½–3	30–35 minutes
Oats	2½	1 hour
Wholewheat	3	1½ hours

Buckwheat Spaghetti with Tomato Sauce and Sunflower Seeds
Serves 6

Both buckwheat and wholewheat spaghetti have more flavour and are more filling than regular spaghetti.

1 lb (450g) buckwheat *or* wholewheat spaghetti
1 quantity of tomato sauce (see p. 72)

6 oz (175g) sunflower seeds
2 tablespoons (30 ml) soya sauce

Preheat oven to 450°F (230°C, gas mark 8). Cook the buckwheat spaghetti according to the manufacturer's instructions or until it is *al dente* (about 15 minutes) in plenty of boiling salted water and then drain. While the spaghetti is cooking heat the prepared tomato sauce in a saucepan and also mix the sunflower seeds with the soya sauce and spread them on a lightly greased baking tray. Bake the sunflower seeds in the hot oven for about 10 minutes. Serve the hot spaghetti covered with tomato sauce and topped with the soya-roasted sunflower seeds.

buckwheat

Vol-au-Vents with Mushroom Filling *Serves 4*

Serve as an hors d'oeuvre, part of a buffet or with vegetables as a main meal.

8 oz (225g) wholemeal puff pastry (see pp. 96–7)
8 oz (225g) mushrooms, finely chopped
2 tablespoons (30 ml) vegetable oil
1 teaspoon (5 ml) lemon juice

1 tablespoon wholemeal flour
3 fl oz (75 ml) soya milk diluted with the same volume of water
1 tablespoon (15 ml) soya sauce
chopped fresh parsley to garnish

Preheat oven to 450°F (230°C, gas mark 8). Roll out two thirds of the pastry ½ in (1 cm) thick and the other third ¼ in (5 mm) thick. Cut rounds of 2 in (5 cm) diameter with a plain or fluted cutter from each portion of pastry. Then from the thick rounds use a smaller cutter to stamp out the centres (these are the lids). Damp the edges of the thin rounds and lay one of the thick pastry rings on top of each one. Lay these and the lids separately on a baking sheet, brush with a little soya milk and bake for 30 minutes in the hot oven.

Cook the mushrooms in the oil and lemon juice gently in a covered pan for 10 minutes. Stir in the flour and cook for a further 2 minutes. Slowly add the soya milk and soya sauce, and when the mixture has thickened cook it for a further 10 minutes, not letting it stick to the bottom of the pan. Spoon portions of the mixture into the cooked vol-au-vent cases, garnish with a little parsley and put the lids on. If the cases or lids have been made ahead of time and they have cooled, warm them through in a hot oven before filling.

Leek and Kasha Pie *Serves 4*

Kasha is the roasted form of buckwheat. For roasting method see p. 42. Cook it with twice its own volume of water for 20–30 minutes.

1 medium onion, chopped
4 large leeks, green part cut off, washed carefully and sliced
1 teaspoon chopped fresh thyme *or* ½ teaspoon dried thyme
1 teaspoon chopped fresh marjoram *or* ½ teaspoon dried marjoram
1 bay leaf
2 tablespoons (30 ml) vegetable oil

8 oz (225g) cooked kasha (4 oz (100g) raw kasha)
1 clove garlic
4 oz (100g) tofu
¼ pint (150 ml) white sauce (see p. 73)
2 tablespoons (30 ml) soya sauce
1 oz (25g) vegan 'cheese' (see p. 77), grated
1 oz (25g) wholemeal breadcrumbs

Preheat oven to 400°F (200°C, gas mark 6). Sauté the onion, leeks, thyme, marjoram and the bay leaf in the oil in a covered saucepan for 10 minutes. Line the base of a greased casserole dish with the mixture and put the cooked kasha on top. Put the garlic, tofu, white sauce and soya sauce in the blender and liquidize for 2 minutes. Pour this mixture over the kasha and top with the vegan cheese and bread-crumbs mixed together. Bake for 40 minutes in the hot oven.

Bulgar Wheat, Vegetable and Bean Casserole   *Serves 4*

This casserole contains a good combination of complementary food stuffs. It provides a complete meal if served with a green salad.

8 oz (225g) bulgar wheat
¾ pint (450 ml) water
1 medium onion, chopped
2 tablespoons (30 ml) vegetable oil
1 carrot, scrubbed and sliced
1 green pepper, seeded, cored and chopped
4 oz (100g) mushrooms, coarsely chopped

3 tomatoes, scalded, peeled and chopped
1 tablespoon tomato purée
2 tablespoons (30 ml) soya sauce
4 oz (100g) of a single bean *or* a bean mix, soaked and cooked until tender, then drained

Lightly dry roast the bulgar wheat in a heavy pan, then add the water, cover and simmer for 15 minutes or until the bulgar is just tender. Remove from the heat. Preheat oven to 400°F (200°C, gas mark 6). Sauté the onion in the vegetable oil in an ovenproof pan or casserole dish for 2 minutes. Add the carrot, cover and cook over a moderate heat until the carrot is softened (about 10 minutes). Add the green pepper and mushrooms, cook for a further 2 minutes. Remove the pan from the heat and stir in the tomatoes, tomato purée and soya sauce, then the bulgar wheat and beans. Bake for 20–30 minutes in the hot oven.

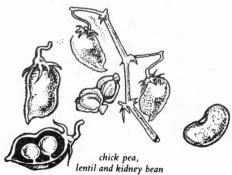

chick pea,
lentil and kidney bean

RICE.

Rice and Buckwheat Rissoles

Makes 12 rissoles

These rissoles are good on their own as a snack or in picnics; served with vegetables they make a fine main course.

1 large onion, chopped
1 teaspoon chopped fresh mixed
  herbs *or* ½ teaspoon dried herbs
2 tablespoons (30 ml) vegetable oil
1½ teaspoons yeast extract
4 oz (100g) cooked rice

4 oz (100g) cooked buckwheat
2 oz (50g) hazelnuts, roasted and
  ground
2 oz (50g) peanuts, roasted and
  ground
vegetable oil for shallow frying

Sauté the onion and herbs in the oil in a pan for 5 minutes. Remove from the heat and dissolve the yeast extract in the mixture. Transfer the mixture to a bowl, add the rice, buckwheat and nuts and mix together very well. Mould the mixture into twelve small, flat, oval shapes for shallow frying or roll into thick, small sausage shapes for deep frying. Shallow or deep fry the rissoles until golden brown. Drain and serve.

Sage, Millet and Nut Bake

Serves 4

As an alternative to the mixed nuts given in the ingredients for this recipe you could substitute pine kernels. Apart from baking, the mixture can also be formed into rissoles which are then shallow fried. Serve with vegetables and a sauce.

2 onions, chopped
1 teaspoon chopped fresh sage *or*
  ½ teaspoon dried sage
2 tablespoons (30 ml) vegetable oil
6 oz (175g) cooked millet (3 oz
  (75g) raw millet)

6 oz (175g) mixed nuts, ground
2 teaspoons yeast extract
1 tablespoon soya flour

Preheat oven to 400°F (200°C, gas mark 6). Sauté the onion and sage in the vegetable oil in a pan for 5 minutes. Stir in the millet and cook for a few minutes. Remove from the heat and add the nuts, yeast extract and soya flour. Mix well. Spoon the mixture into a pie dish and bake for 40 minutes in the hot oven.

Curried Rice and Sosmix Patties   *Makes 12 patties*

We rarely use textured vegetable protein because it seems unaesthetic and takes a large amount of energy to produce. Sosmix is good for a change, however, and is very versatile. This is our favourite recipe.

1 lb (450g) onions, chopped
6 oz (175g) carrot, grated
2 tablespoons chopped fresh mixed herbs *or* 2 teaspoons dried mixed herbs (mostly rosemary)
2 tablespoons (30 ml) vegetable oil
2 teaspoons yeast extract

12 oz (350g) cooked brown rice (6 oz (175g) raw brown rice)
½ teaspoon curry powder
1 teaspoon kelp powder
1 large pack Sosmix, soaked

Preheat oven to 450°F (230°C, gas mark 8). Sauté the onions, carrot and herbs in the oil in a pan for 5 minutes. Transfer to a mixing bowl and add the yeast extract, cooked rice, curry and kelp powders and pre-soaked Sosmix and mix well. Mould the mixture into oval, circular patties, put them onto a lightly greased baking tray and bake for 30 minutes in the hot oven. Turn the patties over halfway through baking.

Onion and Oat Roast   *Serves 4*

Serve this roast as a 'Sunday dinner' with sprouts, jacket potatoes and miso gravy.

2 large onions, chopped
1 oz (25g) margarine *or* 1 tablespoon (15 ml) oil
2 oz (50g) rolled oats

1 teaspoon yeast extract
1 teaspoon dried mixed herbs
4 oz (100g) soya cheese (see p. 77)
a little soya milk

Preheat oven to 350°F (180°C, gas mark 4). Cook the onions in the margarine or oil for 5 minutes over a low heat. Add the rolled oats, yeast extract, herbs and grated soya cheese. Mix well, using a little soya milk if the mixture is too stiff. Bake for 30–40 minutes in a greased baking dish in the preheated oven.

Baked Rice Curry

Serves 4

Serve with stir-fried vegetables or with another vegetable dish.

1 large onion, finely chopped
2 tablespoons (30 ml) vegetable oil
1 lb (450g) cooked long-grain
  brown rice (8 oz (225g) raw
  brown rice)
2 oz (50g) soya cheese, grated
  (see p. 77)

2 tablespoons (30 ml) natural
  tomato ketchup
1½ teaspoons curry powder
1 small teaspoon mustard
sea salt to taste

Preheat oven to 350°F (180°C, gas mark 4). Sauté the onion in the vegetable oil over a low heat for 7 minutes. Remove from the heat and add the cooked rice, cheese, tomato ketchup, curry powder, mustard and sea salt. Put the mixture into a greased baking dish and bake for 30–40 minutes in the preheated oven.

Spanish Rice Ring

Serves 6

2 tablespoons (30 ml) vegetable oil
1 onion, chopped
1 small green pepper, cored,
  seeded and diced
1 small red pepper, cored, seeded
  and diced
½ teaspoon chopped fresh thyme *or*
  ¼ teaspoon dried thyme
6 oz (175g) long-grain brown rice,
  washed

¼ pint (150 ml) dry white wine
½ pint (275 ml) vegetable stock
1 teaspoon agar agar
sea salt to taste

Garnish
2 tomatoes, diced
4 tablespoons chopped parsley
12 olives, stoned and chopped

Heat the oil in a saucepan over a low heat. Add the onion, peppers and thyme and cook gently for 5 minutes. Stir in the rice, wine and vegetable stock. Bring to the boil, cover and simmer for 30 minutes. Preheat oven to 350°F (180°C, gas mark 4). Season, sprinkle the agar agar on the mixture and stir it in. Transfer the mixture to a greased, ring-shaped mould, lined with silver foil, and bake for 20 minutes in the preheated oven. Turn the ring out and serve it garnished with a mixture of the tomatoes, parsley and olives.

Kasha Turnovers

Makes 15 turnovers

Kasha is dry-roasted buckwheat and makes a delicious and nutritious filling for these small pasties. Serve them with a sauce (see pp. 72–5) and salad.

4 tablespoons (60 ml) olive oil
1 large onion, finely chopped
1 clove garlic, crushed
1 teaspoon chopped thyme *or*
  ½ teaspoon dried thyme
8 oz (225g) mushrooms, chopped

¼ teaspoon kelp powder
8 oz (225g) cooked kasha
soya sauce to taste
12 oz (350g) shortcrust *or* flaky
  pastry (see pp. 96 and 97)

Preheat oven to 375°F (190°C, gas mark 5). To make the filling, heat the oil in a large saucepan and sauté the onion, garlic and thyme for 2 minutes. Add the mushrooms and kelp powder and cook for a further 2 minutes. Stir in the kasha and heat through. Season with soya sauce. Roll out the pastry to ⅛ in (2·5 mm) thick and cut it out into approximately 4 in (10 cm) circles. Place a heaped tablespoonful of the mixture on each circle. Fold each to form a half-moon and pinch the edges together after brushing with water. Place the turnovers on a greased baking sheet and bake for 35–40 minutes in the preheated oven or until golden brown.

Pinekernel and Millet Pie

Serves 4

Millet is an excellent grain, easy to cook, nutritious and tasty, but for some reason it is not at all popular in Britain. Pinekernels are delicious when cooked and give this dish a very special flavour.

Pastry
4 oz (100g) margarine
6 oz (175g) wholemeal flour
3 oz (75g) millet flakes
2–3 fl oz (50–75 ml) cold water

Filling
3 tablespoons (45 ml) vegetable oil
4 medium onions, chopped
4 oz (100g) pinekernels, crushed
2 oz (50g) millet flakes
1 dessertspoon yeast extract
½ teaspoon dried sage

To make the pastry rub the margarine into the flour and millet, then mix in enough water to make a workable dough. Roll out two thirds of it and line a 9 in (23 cm) pie dish. Preheat oven to 400°F (200°C, gas mark 6).

For the filling, heat the oil in a saucepan and sauté the onions and pinekernels for 7 minutes. Stir in the millet flakes, yeast extract and sage. Transfer the filling to the pastry case and roll out the remaining pastry for the top. Place the top in position and seal the edges with a fork. Prick the top and bake the pie for 45 minutes in the preheated oven.

Bulgar Wheat Paella

Serves 6

12 oz (350g) bulgar wheat
2 tablespoons (30 ml) vegetable oil
1 large onion, chopped
1 clove garlic, crushed
2 teaspoons chopped fresh basil *or* 1 teaspoon dried basil
1 large carrot, scrubbed and cut into rounds
1 green pepper, cored, seeded and chopped
14 oz (400g) canned tomatoes, drained and chopped (reserve juice)
4 oz (100g) mushrooms, quartered
½ teaspoon kelp powder
water to make tomato juice up to 1 pint (0·5 litre)
soya sauce to taste
2 tablespoons chopped parsley to garnish

Roast the bulgar wheat in a dry pan over a low heat, stirring occasionally, until golden brown (about 5 minutes). Put the bulgar wheat aside and heat the oil in another large pan. Sauté the onion, garlic and basil for 2 minutes over a low heat. Add the carrot, pepper, tomatoes and mushrooms. Stir well. Cover and cook for a further 5 minutes. Stir in the bulgar wheat, kelp powder, tomato juice and water. Bring to the boil, reduce heat, cover and simmer for 20 minutes. Add soya sauce to taste and serve garnished with parsley.

maize

Bean, Pea and Lentil Recipes

Beans, peas and lentils, as a group, are known as pulses or legumes. They are the seeds of plants belonging to the Leguminosae family and, together with cereal grains, they are the earliest and, still to this day, one of man's most important food crops. They provide an excellent source of protein, carbohydrate, vitamin and mineral food and, eaten in combination with grains, provide all our essential amino acids. Leguminous plants return valuable nitrates to the soil and they are one of the most efficient and important substitutes for animal farming.

Beans, peas and lentils are nearly always sold in their dried form and they need to be well soaked, preferably overnight, before cooking. They are then drained, covered in fresh water, brought to the boil, covered and simmered until tender. For more detailed information on the different types of pulses available, cooking times and cooking tips, see *Protein-Rich Vegetarian Cookery* by David Scott* or one of the cookery books now available devoted only to the cooking of meals containing pulses.

The recipes given here cover a wide range of the types of dishes that can be prepared with pulses. The dip recipes given earlier in the book also contain a number of bean dips.

Butterbeans Topped with Basil and Tomato Sauce
Serves 4

½ lb (225g) butterbeans, soaked overnight
2 medium onions, chopped
1 large clove garlic, finely chopped
2 teaspoons chopped fresh basil *or* 1 teaspoon dried basil
3 tablespoons (45 ml) vegetable oil
14 oz (400g) canned tomatoes, drained and chopped (reserve juice)
¼ teaspoon kelp powder
1 tablespoon (30 ml) natural tomato ketchup (e.g. the Whole Earth brand)
2 teaspoons miso
soya sauce to taste
chopped fresh parsley to garnish

* David Scott, *Protein-Rich Vegetarian Cookery*, Rider, 1991.

Drain the butterbeans, cover them with fresh water and boil, covered, until they are just soft (about 1½ hours). Meanwhile, sauté the onions, garlic and basil in the oil in a large pan. Add the tomatoes, kelp, ketchup and juice from the tomatoes to taste and bring to a low boil. Mix the miso to a paste with some of the hot liquid from the pan and stir it in. Add soya sauce to taste. Combine the beans, drained, with the sauce, top with lots of chopped parsley and serve.

Aduki Bean Roll   *Serves 6–8*

This is an unusual way of serving beans, and the pastry looks very appetizing when it comes hot and golden brown from the oven.

1 large onion, sliced
2 cloves garlic, crushed
2 tablespoons (30 ml) vegetable oil
8 oz (225g) mushrooms, sliced
6 oz (175g) aduki beans, soaked,
  cooked and drained

4 oz (100g) ground almonds
sea salt to taste
7 oz (200g) flaky pastry (see
  p. 97)

Sauté the onions and garlic in the vegetable oil in a pan for 10 minutes. Add the mushrooms, cover and continue cooking for a further 10 minutes. Put the contents of the pan into a blender with the aduki beans, almonds and salt to taste and liquidize until smooth.

Preheat oven to 400°F (200°C, gas mark 6). Roll out the pastry into a long oblong 18 × 10 in (45 × 25 cm). Place the filling in a strip along one side, leaving a 1 in (2·5 cm) margin. Fold the other side over and stick it down with a little cold water. Lift the roll onto a greased baking tray. Bake for 35 minutes in the hot oven.

For a special occasion make this roll into a plait by dividing the pastry into three strips. Fill and seal each strip and then plait them together.

Minted Field Bean Hotpot   *Serves 4*

Field beans are the cheapest of beans to buy, but just as nutritious as other beans and locally grown, too.

2 onions, chopped
2 cloves garlic, crushed
1 stick celery, chopped
2 tablespoons (30 ml) vegetable oil
3 large carrots, diced
2 small turnips, diced
2 large tomatoes, skinned and chopped
3 tablespoons chopped fresh mint or 1½ teaspoons dried mint

2 tablespoons (30 ml) soya sauce
1 lb (450g) cooked field beans (reserve cooking liquid) (8 oz (225g) uncooked dried beans)
16 fl oz (450 ml) vegetable stock *or* bean cooking liquid
1 teaspoon miso
1 lb (450g) potatoes, peeled, parboiled and sliced

Sauté the onions, garlic and celery in the vegetable oil in a saucepan. Stir in the carrots and turnips and cook for a few more minutes. Add the tomatoes, mint, soya sauce, beans and vegetable stock. Cover and cook over a moderate heat for 20 minutes. Dissolve the miso in a little of the hot juice and mix it in. Preheat the oven to 400°F (200°C, gas mark 6). Transfer the mixture to an ovenproof dish or casserole dish. Arrange the rounds of potato on top and brush them with a little oil. Bake for about 1 hour in the hot oven.

Sprouted Soya Beans and Vegetables   *Serves 4*

Use a commercial beansprouter or a jam jar to sprout the soya beans. Soak them well first, then water and drain them twice a day until about 1 in (2·5 cm) long. Alternatively, use ordinary beansprouts now available in many health-food stores and at Chinese grocery stores.

1 large onion, chopped
3 tablespoons (45 ml) vegetable oil
3 large carrots, scrubbed and diced
1 lb (450g) courgettes, sliced
4 oz (100g) mushrooms, halved or quartered
1 tablespoon wholemeal flour

8 oz (225g) tomatoes, quartered
¼ pint (150 ml) vegetable stock *or* water and Vecon
sea salt to taste
4 oz (100g) sprouted soya beans *or* regular beansprouts

Sauté the onions in the oil in a saucepan for 5 minutes, then add the carrots, cover and cook over a moderate heat for a further 5 minutes. Stir in the courgettes and mushrooms and cook for a further 10 minutes. Sprinkle the flour over the vegetables and stir well. Add the tomatoes and stock and cook gently for a few minutes. Stir in the sprouted soya beans or beansprouts for the last minute and serve.

Chick Pea, Butterbean and Tahini Casserole   *Serves 4*

This casserole is simple to prepare and is very tasty and nutritious.

2 medium onions, chopped
2 cloves garlic, crushed
2 tablespoons (30 ml) vegetable oil
1 tablespoon tahini
8 oz (225g) chick peas, soaked and cooked, *or* 1 lb (450g) tinned chick peas, drained
4 oz (100g) butterbeans, soaked and cooked, *or* 8 oz (225g) tinned butterbeans, drained

1 lb (450g) tomatoes, skinned and chopped
¼ teaspoon grated nutmeg
2 teaspoons chopped fresh basil *or* 1 teaspoon dried basil
1 large pinch Aramé seaweed (optional)
sea salt to taste

Preheat oven to 350°F (180°C, gas mark 4). Sauté the onions and garlic gently in the oil in a frying pan for 5 minutes. Put them in a casserole dish with the tahini, chick peas, butterbeans, tomatoes, nutmeg, basil, seaweed, salt to taste, and mix well. Cover and cook for 45 minutes in the hot oven.

Blackeye Beanburgers in Tomato Sauce   *Serves 4*

This is a vegan improvement on meatballs in tomato sauce.

8 oz (225g) cooked blackeye beans (reserve cooking liquid) (4 oz (100g) uncooked dried beans)
4 oz (100g) ground hazelnuts
1 teaspoon Vecon (or other yeast extract)
8 oz (225g) tinned tomatoes

2–3 oz (50–75g) wholemeal breadcrumbs
1 tablespoon tahini
sea salt to taste
16 fl oz (450 ml) tomato sauce (see p. 72)

Preheat oven to 350°F (180°C, gas mark 4). Place the beans, hazelnuts and Vecon in blender. Strain the tomatoes and add them to the blender. Liquidize until smooth; add a little bean cooking water if needed to keep the blades moving. Transfer the mixture to a bowl and mix in the breadcrumbs, tahini and salt to taste. Add more bread-crumbs if the mixture is not firm enough to hold together. Form into balls about 2 in (5 cm) in diameter and place them individually onto a greased baking sheet. Bake for 30 minutes in the hot oven. Serve with the tomato sauce reheated.

Spiced Lentil Patties with Coconut Sauce

Makes 10 patties

8 oz (225g) red lentils, cooked tender in ½ pint (275 ml) water
½ teaspoon ground paprika
½ teaspoon ground turmeric
½ teaspoon ground coriander
¼ teaspoon ground ginger

sea salt
vegetable oil for shallow frying
¾ pint (450 ml) tomato sauce (see p. 72)
1 oz (25g) creamed coconut, chopped

Mash the lentils while still hot from cooking with the spices and salt. When cool, form the mixture into 10 circular flattish patties and shallow fry them 3 minutes each side. Heat the tomato sauce and coconut together until the coconut is dissolved. Serve the sauce with the patties.

Aduki Bean Shepherd's Pie

Serves 4–6

2 tablespoons (30 ml) vegetable oil
1 large onion, chopped
1 clove garlic, crushed
4 oz (100g) Jerusalem artichokes *or* potatoes, scrubbed and chopped
2 oz (50g) mushrooms, chopped
8 oz (225g) tinned tomatoes, drained and chopped
12 oz (350g) aduki beans, soaked, cooked tender and drained

1 tablespoon chopped parsley
1 teaspoon dried mixed herbs
2 tablespoons miso
sea salt to taste

Topping
1½ lb (700g) mashed potato
2 oz (50g) vegan 'cheese' (see p. 77)
parsley to garnish

Heat the oil in a saucepan and sauté the onion and garlic for 5 minutes. Add the artichokes or potatoes, cover and cook over a low heat for a further 10 minutes. (Add a little stock or water if needed to stop burning.) Put in the mushrooms and cook for 2 more minutes. Add the tomatoes, beans, parsley and mixed herbs. Bring the mixture to the boil and simmer for 10 minutes. Dissolve the miso in a little of the hot juices and stir in. Add a little sea salt if necessary. Preheat oven to 400°F (200°C, gas mark 6). Transfer the mixture to an ovenproof dish or casserole. Top the beans and vegetables with the mashed potato and sprinkle grated vegan cheese and parsley over the top. Bake for 35 minutes in the hot oven.

Vegetable, Bean and Chestnut Hotpot   *Serves 4*

The chestnuts impart a rich flavour to what can otherwise be an ordinary dish. If you have time, cook the broad beans, cauliflower, green pepper and mushrooms separately, so they have some 'bite' left in them. Serve with hot herb bread (see pp. 76–7) and coleslaw.

1 large onion, chopped
2 teaspoons chopped fresh mixed herbs *or* 1 teaspoon dried herbs
1 bay leaf
3 tablespoons (45 ml) vegetable oil
1 large carrot, scrubbed and chopped
1 stick celery, chopped
¼ each of medium turnip and swede, diced
½ medium parsnip, diced
2 oz (50g) fresh broad beans, optional

1 green pepper, seeded and chopped
4 oz (100g) cauliflower florets
2 oz (50g) mushrooms
8 oz (225g) tomatoes
1 tablespoon tomato purée
12 oz (350g) single type of bean *or* bean stew mix, soaked overnight
2 oz (50g) dried chestnuts, soaked overnight, drained and halved
1 clove garlic
2 tablespoons (30 ml) soya sauce
2 tablespoons chopped parsley
sea salt to taste

Sauté the onion, herbs and bay leaf in the oil in a pressure cooker or large saucepan. After 5 minutes add the carrot, celery, turnip, swede, parsnip, broad beans, pepper, cauliflower and mushrooms. Cover and cook gently for 10 minutes, stirring occasionally. Stir in the tomatoes, tomato purée, soaked beans and chestnuts and just cover with water. Put on the lid and pressure cook for 25 minutes or, in the regular pan, covered, for 1 hour. Open up the cooker, ladle some hot juice into the blender and add the garlic, soya sauce and parsley. Liquidize for 2 minutes and pour back into the stew. Season to taste with salt and serve.

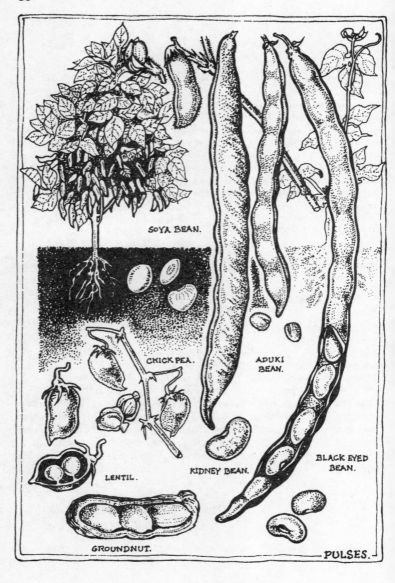

SOYA BEAN.

CHICK PEA.

ADUKI BEAN.

LENTIL.

KIDNEY BEAN.

BLACK EYED BEAN.

GROUNDNUT.

PULSES.

Blackeye Bean and Tomato Pie   *Serves 6*

6 oz (175g) shortcrust pastry
2 tablespoons (30 ml) vegetable oil
1 large onion, chopped
1 teaspoon chopped fresh rosemary
   or ½ teaspoon dried rosemary
1 teaspoon chopped fresh basil *or*
   ½ teaspoon dried basil

1 large carrot, scrubbed and
   chopped
2 oz (50g) blackeye beans, soaked
   and cooked
14 oz (400g) tinned tomatoes,
   drained and chopped
2 tablespoons (30 ml) soya sauce

Preheat oven to 400°F (200°C, gas mark 6). Roll out half the pastry and line a 9 in (23 cm) pie dish with it. Heat the oil in a frying pan and sauté the onion, rosemary and basil for 5 minutes. Add the carrot, cover and cook for a further 5 minutes. Transfer the contents of the pan to the pastry case. Put the beans on top, then the tomatoes, and lastly the soya sauce. Roll out the other half of the pastry and cover the pie. Seal the edges with the tines of a fork and make one or two steam holes in the pastry case. Bake for 40 minutes in the hot oven.

Falafel   *Serves 4–6*

These are spiced chick-pea balls, fried golden brown. Serve with wedges of lemon, salad and pitta bread.

1 lb (450g) chick peas, soaked for
   24 hours, drained
3 cloves garlic
2 teaspoons ground coriander
2 teaspoons ground cumin

2 tablespoons chopped parsley
sea salt to taste
oil to fry (½ in (1 cm) in a frying
   pan)

Put a quarter of the chick peas into a blender with the garlic, coriander, cumin and parsley. Liquidize and keep adding a few more chick peas and then blending until they are all in. You will need to add some water to get them to liquidize but use as little as possible. Season with salt and transfer to a bowl. Form dessertspoonfuls of the mixture into round balls. Heat the oil in a frying pan and fry the falafel for 2–3 minutes or until golden brown all over. Drain well and serve.

Tofu Burgers

Makes 4 burgers

This is a more nutritious and tastier burger than the ubiquitous hamburger.

1 large onion, finely chopped
2 tablespoons (30 ml) vegetable oil
  for shallow frying
1 clove garlic, crushed
1 tablespoon (15 ml) soya sauce

1 teaspoon (5 ml) lemon juice
1 tablespoon wholemeal flour
2 packs tofu, drained
fine wholemeal breadcrumbs for
  coating

Sauté the onion in 2 tablespoons vegetable oil in a frying pan for 5 minutes. Put the onion in a bowl with the garlic, soya sauce, lemon juice and flour. Mash in the tofu. Form the mixture into small burger shapes, coat them in the breadcrumbs and shallow fry in hot oil for 4 minutes on each side.

Green Lentil Wholewheat Lasagne

Serves 6

1 large onion, chopped
3 cloves garlic, crushed
2 tablespoons (30 ml) vegetable oil
12 oz (350g) green lentils, soaked
14 oz (400g) canned tomatoes,
  drained and chopped (reserve
  juice)

1 pint (0.5 litre) water *or* stock (use
  juice from can as part of this)
1 teaspoon garam masala
sea salt to taste
6 oz (175g) wholewheat lasagne
4 oz (100g) hazelnuts, roasted and
  ground

Sauté the onion and garlic in the oil in a saucepan for 10 minutes. Stir in the lentils and tomatoes and pour in the water or stock. Bring to the boil, cover and simmer for 45 minutes. Mix in the garam masala and sea salt to taste. Remove from the heat. Strain off the liquid and reserve. Cook the lasagne according to manufacturer's instructions (or for about 15 minutes) and drain. Preheat oven to 400°F (200°C, gas mark 6). Using a greased shallow baking dish, and starting and finishing with the lentil mixture, layer the lasagne with the lentils. Pour the reserved liquid over gently. Top with the ground hazelnuts and bake for 45 minutes in the hot oven.

Spiced Vegetable and Lentil Roast   *Serves 4*

Couscous gives this savoury a lovely light texture but, if you do not have it, you can use flour, breadcrumbs or any other grain to give more body.

5 oz (150g) red lentils, washed
1 medium onion, chopped
1 medium carrot, scrubbed and
  chopped
1 stick celery, scrubbed and
  chopped
½ teaspoon ground cumin

½ teaspoon ground coriander
¼ teaspoon ground turmeric
sea salt to taste
1 oz (25g) couscous
½ teaspoon yeast extract
2 oz (50g) wholemeal breadcrumbs
1 oz (25g) vegetable margarine

Put the lentils, onion, carrot, celery, cumin, coriander, turmeric and salt in a saucepan. Just cover with water, bring to the boil, cover and simmer for 30 minutes, stirring occasionally. Sprinkle in the couscous and cook for a further 5 minutes. Preheat oven to 400°F (200°C, gas mark 6). Transfer the contents of the pan to an ovenproof dish or casserole dish and spread the yeast extract over the mixture. Cover with breadcrumbs and dot with margarine. Bake for 30–45 minutes in the hot oven.

Soya Bean, Ginger and Potato Layers   *Serves 6*

1 tablespoon (15 ml) vegetable oil
12 oz (350g) tomatoes, sliced
12 oz (350g) soya beans, soaked
  and cooked
1 small onion, grated *or* chopped
  finely
1 clove garlic, crushed

1 stick celery, chopped finely
1 in (2·5 cm) piece stem ginger,
  peeled and chopped
1 lb (450g) potatoes, peeled and
  sliced
3 tablespoons (45 ml) soya sauce
1 oz (25g) vegetable margarine

Oil a casserole dish and put half the tomatoes in the bottom, then a layer of some of the soya beans. Mix the onion, garlic, celery and ginger together and spread some of the mixture evenly over the beans. Cover with a layer of potatoes. Keep layering the beans, tomatoes and potatoes, finishing with the potatoes. Sprinkle the soya sauce over, dot with margarine and bake for 45 minutes, covered, at 375°F (190°C, gas mark 5). Uncover and continue baking for another 45 minutes.

Lentil Flan

4 oz (100g) shortcrust pastry
2 medium onions, chopped
2 tablespoons (30 ml) vegetable oil
1 teaspoon chopped fresh
   marjoram *or* ½ teaspoon dried
   marjoram

2 teaspoons yeast extract
14 oz (400g) red lentils, washed
½ teaspoon kelp powder
¾ pint (425 ml) water
3 medium tomatoes, sliced

Roll out pastry to line a 9 in (23 cm) flan dish. Sauté the onions with the marjoram in the oil for 5 minutes in a saucepan. Add the yeast extract, then the lentils and kelp. Add the water, bring to the boil, cover and cook gently for 25 minutes, stirring occasionally. Preheat oven to 400°F (200°C, gas mark 6). Spread the lentil mixture in the lined flan dish, decorate with slices of tomato and bake for 20–30 minutes in the hot oven.

peas

Nut and Seed Recipes

Nuts and seeds are delicious, highly concentrated foods with a wide range of uses in cooking. They are valuable sources of protein, vitamins, minerals, fats and fibre. For cooking purposes raw nuts or seeds are generally used but for garnishing dishes or for adding to cold foods, such as muesli, they should be lightly roasted to bring out their flavour. Seeds such as sesame and sunflower are a little cheaper than whole nuts; broken nuts, however, are cheap and perfectly good for most cooking purposes. Some of the recipes given here call for roasted and ground or coarsely chopped nuts. Always remember in these cases to roast the nuts before grinding them.

Oven and pan roasting nuts and seeds

Preheat the oven to 375°F (190°C, gas mark 5). Spread the nuts or seeds on an ungreased baking sheet and place them in the oven. Roast them for about 5 minutes or until lightly browned. Shake the nuts or seeds around once or twice during this time. To pan roast, put the nuts or seeds in an ungreased heavy frying pan and gently toss them over a moderate flame until lightly browned all over.

Grinding and chopping nuts and seeds

Grinding nuts or seeds is most easily done with an electric grinder or blender but a manual grain grinder or even a well-cleaned meat grinder with a fine mesh is suitable. For coarsely ground nuts or seeds put a small amount at a time into an electric grinder or blender and switch the machine on for a few seconds only. For more finely ground nuts or seeds leave the machine on for longer. Alternatively, for small quantities use a pestle and mortar or put the nuts or seeds in a clean cloth and roll them with a rolling pin.

To slice nuts, cut them individually with a sharp knife. If they are very hard, soften them by boiling them for a minute or two.

Tomato and Nut Balls *Serves 4*

These savoury nut balls are quick to prepare since they are served uncooked. They are good with a salad and pitta bread. They may also be served with a vegan cheese sauce.

1 medium onion, finely chopped
1 small clove garlic, finely chopped
2 tablespoons (30 ml) vegetable oil
8 oz (225g) tomatoes, skinned and chopped
4 oz (100g) hazel *or* Brazil nuts, ground *or* coarsely crushed

6 oz (175g) wholemeal breadcrumbs
salt and freshly milled black pepper to taste
chopped fresh parsley to garnish

Sauté the onion and the garlic in the oil in a pan until softened. Add the tomatoes and cook for another 5 minutes. Pour the mixture into a bowl and add the nuts and breadcrumbs. Mix well. Season to taste with salt and black pepper. Form the mixture into 2 in (5 cm) diameter balls. Cover the tomato and nut balls with masses of chopped parsley.

Mushroom Almond Loaf *Serves 4*

Serve the loaf with vegetables and/or salad and with or without a sauce. It keeps well in a refrigerator and is good hot or cold.

1 large onion, chopped
2 tablespoons (30 ml) vegetable oil
1 lb (450g) mushrooms, finely chopped
2 tablespoons soya flour
4 oz (100g) ground almonds plus a few whole almonds to garnish

10 oz (275g) wholewheat breadcrumbs
1 teaspoon yeast extract
1 teaspoon dried mixed herbs
sea salt to taste
parsley to garnish

Preheat oven to 350°F (180°C, gas mark 4). Sauté the onion for 5 minutes in the vegetable oil in a saucepan. Add the mushrooms and fry for a further 5 minutes. Remove from the heat. Mix in the soya flour, almonds, 8 oz (225g) breadcrumbs, yeast extract, mixed herbs and sea salt. Pack the mixture into a lightly greased 2 lb (900g) loaf tin, the bottom of which is lined with the remaining breadcrumbs, and bake for 1 hour in the hot oven. Loosen the sides of the loaf and turn it out. Decorate the top with whole almonds and parsley and serve.

Sunflower Seed, Herb and Potato Pie   *Serves 4*

4 oz (100g) sunflower seeds,
   roasted and coarsely crushed
4 oz (100g) wholewheat
   breadcrumbs
1 large onion, chopped
3 teaspoons chopped fresh mixed
   herbs *or* 1½ teaspoons dried
   mixed herbs

1 clove garlic, crushed
1½ lbs (700g) potatoes, peeled and
   thinly sliced
2 tablespoons (30 ml) soya sauce
¼ pint (150 ml) soya milk with ¼
   pint (150 ml) water
2 oz (50g) vegetable margarine

Preheat oven to 350°F (180°C, gas mark 4). Mix together in a bowl the sunflower seeds, breadcrumbs, onion, herbs and garlic. Layer the sunflower-seed mixture and the sliced potatoes in a lightly greased baking dish, ending with a layer of potatoes. Combine the soya sauce and soya milk together and pour the mixture over the potatoes. Dot the margarine over the top and bake, covered, for 1½ hours in the hot oven. Uncover and bake for a further 30 minutes.

Mushroom and Hazelnut Croustade   *Serves 4*

A croustade is a sort of upside-down crumble with a sauce on top. It is very tasty.

4 oz (100g) wholemeal
   breadcrumbs
4 oz (100g) hazelnuts, roasted and
   crushed
4 oz (100g) flaked almonds
1 clove garlic, crushed
1 teaspoon chopped fresh mixed
   herbs *or* ½ teaspoon dried mixed
   herbs
2 oz (50g) vegetable margarine

Sauce
1 large onion, chopped
1 lb (450g) mushrooms, chopped
3 tablespoons (45 ml) vegetable oil
2 oz (50g) wholemeal flour
1 tablespoon tahini
3 tablespoons (45 ml) soya sauce
8 fl oz (225 ml) soya milk, diluted
   with 8 fl oz (225 ml) water
2 tablespoons chopped parsley to
   garnish

Preheat oven to 425°F (220°C, gas mark 7). Combine the breadcrumbs, hazelnuts, almonds, garlic and herbs. Mix well and rub in the margarine. Press the mixture down well into a swiss-roll tin. Bake for 20 minutes in the hot oven. Allow to cool and then turn the croustade out.

Sauce
Sauté the onion and mushrooms in the oil for 5 minutes. Stir in the flour and then the tahini and soya sauce; finally stir in the soya milk very slowly. Pour this sauce over the croustade and garnish with parsley.

NUTS.

ALMOND.

HAZEL.

PINE.

WALNUT.

BRAZIL.

CASHEW.

Mushroom, Rosemary and Nutmeat Pie   *Serves 4–6*

This is one of the few recipes in the book that uses a commercial product as a main ingredient. Tinned nutmeat is convenient if you are in a hurry and it is often well liked by children.

1 large onion, sliced
2 tablespoons (30 ml) vegetable oil
2 teaspoons chopped fresh
  rosemary *or* 1 teaspoon dried
  rosemary
1 lb (450g) tomatoes, peeled and
  chopped

1 lb (450g) mushrooms, halved
1 large tin (15 oz (425g)) Nuttolene,
  cut into large chunks
2 tablespoons (30 ml) soya sauce
4 oz (100g) shortcrust pastry (see
  p. 96)

Preheat oven to 400°F (200°C, gas mark 6). Sauté the onion in the oil for 5 minutes in a saucepan. Stir in the rosemary, tomatoes, mushrooms, Nuttolene and soya sauce. Stir and cook a further 2 minutes. Put the mixture into a deep pie dish. Roll out the pastry and cover the dish. Bake for 40 minutes in the hot oven.

Steamed Hazelnut Pudding   *Serves 4*

This is a delicious, moist nut pudding. It takes a long time to cook although it is much quicker in a pressure cooker. Serve with roast potatoes and vegetables for Sunday lunch.

1 medium onion, chopped finely
1 clove garlic, crushed
2 teaspoons chopped fresh
  rosemary *or* 1 teaspoon dried
  rosemary
2 tablespoons (30 ml) vegetable oil
1 teaspoon yeast extract

1 medium carrot, grated
½ teaspoon kelp powder
1 tablespoon soya flour
4 oz (100g) hazelnuts, roasted and
  crushed
2 oz (50g) wholemeal breadcrumbs
3 fl oz (75 ml) cold water

Sauté the onion, garlic and rosemary in the vegetable oil for 5 minutes in a saucepan. Stir in the yeast extract, carrot, kelp, soya flour, hazelnuts, breadcrumbs and water. Mix well and transfer the mixture to a greased pudding basin. (The easiest to use is a plastic one with its own lid.) Steam for 1 hour in a pressure cooker or 2½ hours in a saucepan. Turn the pudding out of the basin and serve.

Chestnut and Rice Roast

Serves 4

This is a traditional Christmas dinner savoury for vegetarians and is delicious with cranberry sauce.

2 tablespoons (30 ml) vegetable oil
1 large onion, chopped
4 oz (100g) cooked brown rice
  (2 oz (50g) raw rice)
8 oz (225g) dried chestnuts, soaked
  overnight and cooked tender

1 tablespoon soya flour
2 teaspoons yeast extract
1 teaspoon chopped fresh sage *or*
  ½ teaspoon dried sage

Preheat oven to 375°F (190°C, gas mark 5). Heat the oil in a saucepan and cook the onion gently for 5 minutes. Add the rice, chestnuts, soya flour, yeast extract and sage. Mix together well, transfer the mixture to an ovenproof dish or casserole and bake for 40 minutes in the hot oven.

Pinekernel Roast

Serves 4

Pinekernels (also known as pine nuts and pignolias) are expensive but they have a lovely flavour in a cooked dish. Plain unroasted pine nuts are rather lacking in flavour.

2 large onions, chopped
2 tablespoons (30 ml) vegetable oil
1 teaspoon chopped fresh sage *or*
  ½ teaspoon dried sage
2 tablespoons yeast extract

1 tablespoon soya flour
6 oz (175g) pinekernel nuts,
  ground
3 oz (75g) wholemeal breadcrumbs
sea salt to taste

Preheat oven to 375°F (190°C, gas mark 5). Sauté the onions for 5 minutes in the oil in a saucepan. Add the sage, yeast extract, soya flour, pinekernel nuts and breadcrumbs. Mix well and season with salt. Transfer the mixture to a greased casserole dish and bake for 40 minutes in the hot oven.

pine nuts

Cashew Nut and Lemon Loaf *Serves 8*

2 tablespoons (30 ml) vegetable oil
1 large onion, chopped
2 teaspoons chopped fresh thyme
or 1 teaspoon dried thyme
1 clove garlic, crushed
1 medium carrot, peeled and
grated
grated rind of 1 lemon

12 oz (350g) cashew nuts, roasted
and ground
4 oz (100g) wholemeal
breadcrumbs
1 tablespoon soya flour
sea salt to taste
a little water if necessary

Preheat oven to 375°F (190°C, gas mark 5). Heat the oil in a saucepan. Sauté the onion, thyme and garlic for 5 minutes. Mix in the carrot, lemon rind, cashew nuts, breadcrumbs and soya flour. Season with salt and add a little water if the texture is too thick. Transfer to a 2 lb (900g) loaf tin which has been lined with silver foil, leaving enough foil extending along one side to cover the roast. Bake for 1 hour in the hot oven.

Vegetable Brochettes with Rice and Brazil Nuts *Serves 4*

Although vegetable brochettes are baked in this recipe they are equally good grilled under a hot grill or barbecued over glowing charcoal.

2 courgettes, cut into thick rings
12 large mushrooms, washed and
left whole
4 large tomatoes, cut in half
1 large green pepper, seeded and
cut into 2 in (5 cm) squares
1 large red pepper, seeded and cut
into 2 in (5 cm) squares

a little olive oil
1½ lb (700g) cooked brown rice
(12 oz (350g) raw rice)
4 oz (100g) Brazil nuts, roasted
and coarsely chopped
soya sauce to taste

Preheat oven to 400°F (200°C, gas mark 6). Divide the courgettes, mushrooms, tomatoes, green and red peppers into four heaps. Place four skewers through the vegetables, kebab style. Brush them with olive oil and lay on a greased baking tray. Bake for 40 minutes, turning once. Serve on a bed of hot rice with Brazil nuts sprinkled over. Allow people individually to season their brochettes with soya sauce.

Vegetable Pie with Hazelnut Pastry   *Serves 4*

The flavour of the hazelnut pastry sets off the flavour of the vegetables and lifts this pie out of the ordinary.

4 oz (100g) wholemeal flour
1 oz (25g) hazelnuts, roasted and ground
2 oz (50g) margarine
water to mix
2 tablespoons (30 ml) oil
1 large onion, chopped
1 teaspoon chopped fresh rosemary *or* ½ teaspoon dried rosemary

1 large potato, peeled and chopped
1 carrot, chopped
1 large courgette, cut in rings
8 oz (225g) tinned sweetcorn, drained
8 oz (225g) tomatoes, peeled and chopped
sea salt to taste

Combine the flour and ground hazelnuts and mix well. Rub in the margarine and enough water to form a firm, non-sticky pastry. Wrap the pastry in cling film and set it aside in the refrigerator. Preheat oven to 400°F (200°C, gas mark 6). Heat the oil in a large saucepan. Sauté the onion and rosemary for 5 minutes. Add the potato, carrot, courgette and sweetcorn and cook for a further 5 minutes, adding a little water if necessary to prevent sticking. Finally, add the tomatoes and season with salt. Transfer the filling to a deep pie dish. Roll out the hazelnut pastry to cover the dish and bake in the hot oven for 40 minutes.

Pinekernel Chilled Mould   *Serves 3*

This cold nut mould is lovely on a warm day served with crackers and perhaps a green salad.

1 tablespoon (15 ml) vegetable oil
1 medium onion, chopped
1 teaspoon chopped fresh sage *or* ½ teaspoon dried sage
½ pint (275 ml) stock *or* water with ½ teaspoon yeast extract

1 tablespoon (15 ml) soya sauce
1 teaspoon agar agar
4 oz (100g) ground pinekernels
sea salt to taste

Heat the oil in a saucepan and sauté the onion with the sage for 5 minutes. Add the stock with the soya sauce and bring to the boil. Sprinkle in the agar agar, whisking well. Stir in the pinekernels, season with salt and transfer the mixture to a mould which has been rinsed in cold water. Leave to set in the refrigerator.

Savoury Hazelnut Pastry Roll *Serves 4–6*

8 oz (225g) wholemeal flour
4 oz (100g) hazelnuts, roasted and
  ground
3 oz (75g) margarine
cold water to mix

1–2 teaspoons yeast extract
1 medium carrot, grated
1 onion, finely chopped
2 tablespoons finely chopped
  parsley

Preheat oven to 400°F (200°C, gas mark 6). Combine the flour and hazelnuts and mix well. Rub in the margarine and enough water to form a firm, non-sticky pastry. Roll out the pastry to form an oblong shape ¼ in (5 mm) thick and spread this with the yeast extract. Sprinkle the carrot, onion and parsley over the pastry. Roll the pastry up and prick the top. Place on a greased baking sheet and bake for 30 minutes in the hot oven. Serve hot or cold.

Hazelnut and Vegetable Burgers *Makes 4 burgers*

Served as a hamburger in a wholemeal roll this is delicious, nutritious and filling.

2 carrots, grated
1 onion, finely chopped
2 sticks celery, finely chopped
4 oz (100g) cabbage, finely grated
1 clove garlic, crushed
2 oz (50g) hazelnuts, roasted and
  ground
2 tablespoons wheatgerm
2 tablespoons wholemeal
  breadcrumbs, plus more for
  coating burgers

1 tablespoon soya flour
1 teaspoon dried mixed herbs
sea salt to taste
1 tablespoon (15 ml) soya milk
1 tablespoon tomato purée
2 fl oz (50 ml) water
vegetable oil for frying

Mix together the carrots, onion, celery, cabbage, garlic, nuts, wheatgerm, breadcrumbs, soya flour and herbs. Whisk the soya milk, tomato purée and water together and stir the mixture into the dry ingredients. Season with salt and form the mixture into four burgers. Coat them in breadcrumbs and shallow fry golden brown on both sides or bake on a greased baking sheet for 20–30 minutes in preheated oven at 350°F (180°C, gas mark 4).

Sauces and Spreads

Here is a collection of sauces that go well with vegetable, grain, pulse, nut and seed recipes. Most of them have been referred to as suitable accompaniments for one or more of the dishes mentioned. The tomato sauce is especially versatile and is used in several recipes. The spreads are good for sandwich making, serving with toast or as part of a light meal.

Sauces

Tomato Sauce
Makes 2½ pints (1·4 litres)

This is a tasy and versatile tomato sauce, good with grains, vegetables, beans and as a base for topping pizza.

3 medium onions, chopped
2 cloves garlic, crushed
3 teaspoons chopped fresh thyme
  or 1½ teaspoon dried thyme
2 bay leaves
2 tablespoon (30 ml) vegetable oil
3 medium carrots, scrubbed and
  diced

3 sticks celery, diced
4 oz (100g) mushrooms, quartered
14 oz (400g) tinned tomatoes,
  chopped (reserve juice from tin)
½ teaspoon kelp powder
1 tablespoon tomato purée
1 tablespoon (15 ml) soya sauce
sea salt if necessary

Sauté the onions, garlic, thyme and bay leaves in the vegetable oil for 5 minutes. Add the carrots and celery, together with a little water if the onions are browning. When the vegetables are softened (about 15 minutes) add the mushrooms and tomatoes with the juice from the can. Add the kelp, tomato purée, soya sauce and sea salt. Bring to the boil, cover, reduce heat and cook for 10 minutes. This sauce is naturally chunky; if you wish liquidize it to make it smooth.

Chestnut and Tomato Sauce

Serves 4

Serve this sauce with any grain. It is also delicious blended as a 'Bolognese' sauce on pasta.

1 large onion, finely chopped
1 clove garlic, crushed
1 teaspoon chopped fresh thyme *or*
  ½ teaspoon dried thyme
1 teaspoon chopped fresh rosemary
  or ½ teaspoon dried rosemary
2 tablespoons (30 ml) vegetable oil

12 oz (350g) dried chestnuts,
  soaked in boiling water, left
  overnight and drained
14 oz (400g) canned tomatoes,
  chopped (reserve juice from can)
2 tablespoons (30 ml) soya sauce
½ teaspoon kelp powder

Sauté the onion, garlic, thyme and rosemary in the vegetable oil in a pressure cooker or a large saucepan for 5 minutes. Add the chestnuts, tomatoes with their juice, soya sauce and kelp powder. Just cover with water. Bring up to pressure and cook for 30 minutes; or for 1 hour, covered, in the saucepan. Blend the mixture smooth in a food processor or blender for the 'Bolognese' consistency.

White Sauce

Makes 1 pint (0·5 litre)

1 oz (25g) vegetable margarine
1 oz (25g) wholemeal flour

1 pint (0.5 litre) soya milk
sea salt to taste

Melt the margarine in a saucepan over a low heat. Take the pan off the heat and stir in the flour. Cook for 5 minutes, stirring occasionally to make a roux. Set aside. Warm up the soya milk. Return the roux to medium heat and add a little soya milk. Stir with a wooden spoon until smooth. Continue adding small amounts of soya milk until it has all been used. Stir continuously. Add salt to taste and use as required.

Note: For a fat-free sauce, warm the milk, put it into the liquidizer with the flour, blend for 1 minute. Pour this mixture into a saucepan and bring to the boil, whisking constantly. Turn heat down to simmer and continue to cook for 5 minutes.

'Cheese' Sauce

Makes 1¼ pints (0·7 litre)

1 pint (0·5 litre) soya milk
1 oz (25g) wholemeal flour
1 dessertspoon (10 ml)
  concentrated apple juice

½ teaspoon (2·5 ml) prepared mild
  mustard
3–4 oz (75–100g) soya cheese,
  grated (see p. 77)

Warm the milk in a saucepan to near boiling. Pour it into a liquidizer and blend with the flour, apple juice and mustard for 1 minute. Pour the mixture back into the saucepan and bring to the boil, whisking all the time. Turn down the heat and simmer for 5 minutes. Stir in the soya cheese and use as required.

Miso Gravy   *Makes 1¼ pints (0·7 litre)*

Use this miso gravy in all the ways a conventional gravy would be used.

2 large onions, finely chopped
2 oz (50g) vegetable margarine
1 oz (25g) wholemeal flour

1 pint (0·5 litre) water
1 tablespoon miso

Sauté the onion in the margarine in a saucepan for 15 minutes. Stir in the flour and cook over a low heat for 5 minutes. Slowly add the water, bring to the boil and cook for a further 5 minutes. Dissolve the miso in a little of the hot liquid and return it to the pan. Do not allow to boil again or the enzymes in the miso will be lost. Serve hot.

Split Pea Curry Sauce   *Serves 4*

Serve this sauce over rice or vegetables with rice accompaniment.

8 oz (225g) split peas, soaked and
   cooked until very tender
sea salt to taste
¼ teaspoon ground turmeric
½ teaspoon ground coriander
1 tablespoon desiccated coconut

1 medium onion, chopped
2 tablespoons (30 ml) vegetable oil
¼ teaspoon mustard seeds
¼ teaspoon fennel seeds
½ teaspoon garam masala

Mash the split peas and the salt, turmeric, coriander and coconut. Sauté the onion in the oil in a frying pan with the mustard seeds, fennel seeds and garam masala for about 10 minutes. Add the pea mixture and cook over a low heat for 5 minutes, stirring all the time.

Spicy Beetroot and Tomato Sauce

See recipe for Spicy Beetroot and Tomato Dish, p. 38.

Spreads

Date, Cashew and Lemon Spread   *Makes 14 oz (400g)*

7 oz (200g) cashew nuts, ground
5 oz (150g) dates, finely chopped

6–7 tablespoons (90–105 ml) lemon juice

Combine the ingredients and mix well together. Store unused spread in a glass jar in a cool place.

Banana, Tahini and Honey Spread   *Serves 2*

1 large banana, mashed
2 teaspoons tahini
1 teaspoon honey

Mash the banana, tahini and honey together and use immediately.

Avocado and Honey Spread   *Serves 2*

1 ripe avocado, thinly sliced
honey to taste

Scoop out the avocado flesh and mash it with the honey.

Avocado, Mustard and Tomato Spread   *Serves 2–3*

Use a mild mustard for this. We use Life mustard which has no added salt.

1 avocado, sliced
1 tomato, sliced
2 teaspoons prepared mustard

Layer the avocado, tomato and mustard on slices of wholemeal bread and serve.

Herb Butter and French Bread   *Serves 4–6*

3 teaspoons dried parsley
1 teaspoon dried marjoram
3 cloves garlic, crushed

4 oz (100g) soft vegetable margarine

Preheat oven to 350°F (180°C, gas mark 4). Mash the herbs and garlic into the margarine. Spread the mixture on wholemeal French bread sliced down the middle. Put the two halves of the bread together and wrap in foil. Bake the bread in the hot oven for 20 minutes.

Miso Spread   *Serves 2*

2 tablespoons miso
1 spring onion, chopped
2 teaspoons (10 ml) orange juice

Mash all ingredients together; the spread can be used immediately.

Vegan 'Cheese'   *Makes 8 oz (225g)*

This is a good substitute for ordinary cheese on sandwiches, in omelettes, etc.

3½ oz (75g) Soyolk* flour   1 teaspoon yeast extract (or more
4 oz (100g) hard margarine   to taste)

Melt the margarine in a small bowl, stir in the soya flour and work it until the mixture is smooth. Stir in the yeast extract and leave the cheese to set.

Aduki Bean Spread   *Serves 6*

This spread is good on bread or it can be used as a filling for savoury pasties.

8 oz (225g) cooked aduki beans,   ½ medium onion, finely chopped
   drained   1 clove garlic, crushed
1 tablespoon sesame seeds   salt and black pepper to taste
1 tablespoon (15 ml) vegetable oil
   (sesame oil if possible)

Beat the beans to a paste in an electric blender. Dry roast the sesame seeds in a frying pan or small saucepan until they are lightly browned and start to pop, and combine them with the aduki-bean paste. Heat the oil in a heavy pan and sauté the onion and garlic until golden. Stir in the aduki paste and simmer, stirring, over a low heat for 5 minutes.

* Soyolk is a heat-treated soya flour that can be used uncooked.

Season to taste. If the mixture is too thick add a little bean cooking water or oil in both. Transfer to a bowl and allow to cool.

Variation
Add 1 tablespoon (15 ml) wine vinegar to the spread; it gives it a little extra tang.

Aduki Bean and Chestnut Spread   *Serves 4*

If this spread is made with honey it can be used as a substitute for jam in cake making.

4 oz (100g) cooked aduki beans, drained

4 oz (100g) chestnut purée (available tinned)
salt or honey to taste

Blend or crush the ingredients together, adding salt for a savoury dip or honey for a sweet one. Add some of the water the beans were cooked in if the consistency of the spread is too thick.

Salads and Salad Dressings

Salads are one of the cornerstones of a vegan diet. Raw vegetables and fruit contain all their original nutrients and fibre and lose none through cooking or processing. When possible buy vegetables grown locally and buy them in season. In this way you will get them at their freshest and cheapest, which is a more advantageous way of using seasonal specialities than deep freezing. If you have a source of organically grown vegetables they are, of course, really worth buying. Better flavour and the peace of mind that comes from knowing they are free from pesticides compensate for the extra cost and labour involved in using them.

Salads

Tomato and Onion Salad   *Serves 4*

1 large onion, sliced
vinaigrette dressing (see p. 88)
1 teaspoon dried basil

1 lb (450g) tomatoes, sliced
chopped parsley to garnish

Put the onion in a sieve and pour some boiling water over it. Transfer the onion to a salad bowl and add dressing to taste and the basil. Toss the mixture and then gently stir in the tomatoes. Garnish with parsley and serve.

Nut and Vegetable Rice Salad   *Serves 6*

This salad is good on its own or stuffed in pitta bread.

12 oz (350g) cooked brown rice
4 oz (100g) red cabbage, finely
  chopped *or* grated
1 small green pepper, seeded,
  thinly sliced and chopped

1 small carrot, scrubbed and grated
1 oz (25g) sultanas
1 oz (25g) cashew nut pieces
¼ pint (150 ml) tahini and apple
  dressing (see p. 88)

Combine the rice with the red cabbage, green pepper, carrot, sultanas
and cashew nuts. Pour the dressing over the salad and mix well.

Cold Stuffed Tomatoes   *Serves 4*

2 oz (50g) cashew nuts, ground
1 oz (25g) wholemeal breadcrumbs
1 small clove garlic, crushed
¼ teaspoon curry powder
1 teaspoon Soyolk flour
sea salt to taste
4 large tomatoes, halved and pulp
  removed (reserve pulp)

1 tablespoon (15 ml) cold water
chopped chives *or* chopped parsley
  to garnish
4 lettuce leaves
4 slices lemon

Combine the cashew nuts, breadcrumbs, garlic, curry powder, flour
and salt and mix well. Stir in the tomato pulp and water and fill the
tomato halves with the mixture. Top each with chopped chives or
parsley and serve on a lettuce leaf decorated with a slice of lemon.

Beetroot and Beansprout Salad   *Serves 4*

This is a quick and easy salad to make. Serve it as soon as it is made
otherwise the beetroot colours the beansprouts.

4 oz (100g) beansprouts
1 small beetroot, cooked and sliced
  in semicircles
4 oz (100g) button mushrooms,
  washed

1 green pepper, sliced in rings
¼ pint (150 ml) vinaigrette dressing
  (see p. 88)

Mix the ingredients together in a salad bowl and serve immediately.

Chick Pea Salad in Lemon Dressing *Serves 4–6*

For a quick salad use tinned chick peas; alternatively, next time you cook some chick peas keep some aside to make this salad.

2 tablespoons (30 ml) olive oil	3 tablespoons chopped chives
2 tablespoons (30 ml) lemon juice	sea salt to taste
1 small onion, finely chopped	6 oz (175g) chick peas, soaked,
2 cloves garlic, crushed	cooked and drained

Mix the olive oil with the lemon juice and beat well. Add the onion, garlic, chives and sea salt. Toss the chick peas in this dressing and serve cold.

Avocado, Celery and Apple Salad *Serves 4*

Check the avocado pears are ripe by squeezing them gently between finger and thumb. They should 'give' a little if ready for use. The celery and apple give the salad its 'crunch' so, if possible, use them fresh from the refrigerator.

2 sticks celery, diced	¼ pint (150 ml) tahini and apple
1 small dessert apple, cored and sliced	dressing (see p. 88)
2 medium-sized ripe avocados, peeled, stoned and diced	chopped parsley to garnish

Mix the celery, apple and avocado together. Add the dressing and top with parsley.

Double Beetroot and Apple Salad *Serves 4*

Raw beetroot has a completely different flavour from the cooked variety and this recipe uses both.

1 large beetroot, cooked and grated	1 large dessert apple, grated
1 large beetroot, raw, scrubbed and grated	vinaigrette dressing (see p. 88)

Mix together the cooked and raw beetroot. Add the apple and stir well. Toss in a little vinaigrette dressing (be careful not to use too much as this mixture can easily get too sloppy).

CHIVES.   SPANISH ONION.   WELSH ONION.

Carrot and Apple Salad   *Serves 4*

This is a favourite in our family but the children prefer a vinaigrette dressing. Serve as a starter, side dish or as part of a salad meal.

large carrots, scrubbed and
  coarsely grated
dessert apple, grated
in (7·5 cm) piece of cucumber,
  grated

1 tablespoon chopped fresh mint
¼ pint (150 ml) tahini and apple
  dressing (see p. 88)

Mix together the carrots, apple and cucumber. Add the mint and pour the dressing over the salad. Toss.

Fennel and Orange Salad   *Serves 4*

Like chicory leaves, fennel goes particularly well with orange.

large head fennel, finely chopped
  (including the green part)
large sweet orange, peeled and
  chopped

1 oz (25g) raisins
¼ pint (150 ml) vinaigrette dressing
  (see p. 88)

Mix the fennel, orange and raisins together. Add the vinaigrette dressing and toss well.

New Potato Salad   *Serves 4*

This is a simple salad, particularly successful with the first of the new potatoes.

12 oz (350g) new potatoes
2 tablespoons chopped fresh mint
pint (150 ml) tofu dressing (see
  p. 89)

chopped chives *or* parsley to
  garnish

Cook the potatoes in plenty of salted water. Keep an eye on them and remove the pan from the heat as soon as they are tender (press one between finger and thumb; it should 'give' a little when cooked). Drain the potatoes and rinse them under cold water until cold enough to touch. Dice them and mix them with the mint and dressing. Garnish with chives or parsley.

Kidney Bean and Coconut Salad

Serves

This is a Jamaican-style dish. The coconut gives a rich texture and flavour.

¼ pint (150 ml) boiling water
1 oz (25g) creamed coconut, chopped
1 small onion, grated
2 teaspoons chopped fresh rosemary *or* 1 teaspoon dried rosemary

6 oz (175g) red kidney beans, soaked, cooked and drained
sea salt to taste
a little desiccated coconut to garnish

Pour the boiling water over the coconut, add the onion and rosemary. Toss the kidney beans in the mixture; salt to taste. Allow to cool before garnishing with desiccated coconut and serving.

Parsnip and Date Salad

Serves

We are not sure if parsnips are ever grown in the same areas as dates but they certainly taste well together.

3 large parsnips, grated
8 dates, pour boiling water over them, drain and then chop

1 teaspoon chopped fresh rosemary *or* ½ teaspoon dried rosemary
vinaigrette dressing (see p. 88)

Mix the parsnips, dates and rosemary together. Pour as much vinaigrette over as necessary to suit your taste. Toss and serve.

Three Greens Salad

Serves 6

Three varieties of green vegetables are par-cooked and, while still warm, tossed in vinaigrette dressing. The dressing is absorbed and the salad is then chilled before serving.

2 fl oz (50 ml) water
salt to taste
1 small head cauliflower, cut up into florets
2 courgettes, sliced into rounds

6 oz (175g) French beans, left whole
vinaigrette dressing (see p. 88) to taste

Bring the salted water to the boil in a saucepan. Put the cauliflower in the pan, cover and simmer for 3 minutes. Add the courgettes and beans and simmer for a further 5 minutes. Do not overcook as they are best a little crunchy. Remove the pan from the heat, drain the vegetables and briefly rinse them under the cold tap. Drain them again and transfer them to a salad bowl. Toss in a little vinaigrette dressing. Chill before serving.

Herb and Nut Salad Balls
Serves 4

These salad balls make a lovely and unusual centrepiece for a green salad.

1 large apple, grated
1 large carrot, scrubbed and grated
2 oz (50g) cashew nuts, ground
1 tablespoon chopped fresh chives
1 tablespoon chopped fresh sorrel
  (if not available use ½ teaspoon
  (2·5 ml) lemon juice)
small head of lettuce

Thoroughly mix the apple, carrot, nuts, chives and sorrel together by hand. Form tablespoonful amounts of this mixture into moderately tight-packed balls. Wet your hands if the mixture sticks too much. Serve on a bed of lettuce.

Fig and Walnut Salad
Serves 6

This colourful, crunchy salad is both tasty and nutritious. If fresh figs are available they can be used instead of the dried variety.

½ small white cabbage, finely
  grated
4 medium carrots, scrubbed and
  grated
1 small onion, finely chopped
1 cooking apple, grated
tofu dressing (see p. 89)
4 oz (100g) dried figs, sliced
2 dessert apples, cored and thinly
  sliced
juice of 1 orange
4 oz (100g) walnut halves

Mix together the cabbage, carrots, onion and cooking apple. Add the tofu dressing. Put the mixture in a serving bowl and arrange slices of figs and dessert apples over it, leaving a space in the middle. Pour orange juice over and, lastly, heap the nuts in the middle.

Sweet-and-Sour Cold Stir-Fried Salad   *Serves 2*

The vegetables in this salad are only lightly cooked and should retain some crunch. The vegetables given here are only suggestions and, using the same method, other vegetable combinations may be just as good.

2 tablespoons (30 ml) vegetable oil
1 clove garlic, crushed
1 red pepper, seeded and cut into strips
1 medium onion, sliced
1 medium carrot, peeled and cut into thin rounds

6 oz (175g) white cabbage, finely shredded
3 radishes, sliced
4 oz (100g) beansprouts
1 tablespoon (15 ml) wine vinegar
1 tablespoon clear honey
1 tablespoon (15 ml) soya sauce

Heat the oil in a saucepan and cook the garlic, pepper, onion and carrot, stirring, for 3–4 minutes. Add the cabbage and cook for a further 3 minutes, stirring all the time. Add radishes and beansprouts and cook for 1 minute. Mix the vinegar, honey and soya sauce in a bowl and add the mixture to the pan. Transfer to a serving bowl and allow to cool. Serve.

Caraway Coleslaw with Tofu Dressing   *Serves 4*

The caraway in this dish gives the coleslaw an original flavour. Caraway seeds are also said to aid digestion.

12 oz (350g) white cabbage, grated
3 large carrots, scrubbed and grated
½ small onion, finely chopped

2 oz (50g) sultanas, washed
1 tablespoon caraway seeds
¼ pint (150 ml) tofu dressing (see p. 89)

Mix together in a salad bowl the cabbage, carrots, onion, sultanas and caraway seeds. Pour the dressing over the salad and mix well.

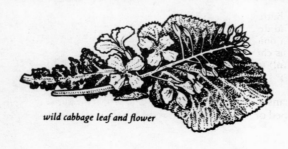

wild cabbage leaf and flower

Red and Green Salad with Grapes

Serves 4

This is a colourful autumn or winter salad.

8 oz (225g) Chinese leaves *or* white cabbage, coarsely chopped
1 small leek, thinly sliced
4 tomatoes, cut into small pieces
1 large red pepper, seeded and cut into rings

4 oz (100g) sweet white grapes, halved and seeded, *or* seedless grapes
vinaigrette dressing (see p. 88)

Mix the Chinese leaves and leek together and put the mixture in the bottom of a shallow serving bowl. Spread the tomatoes and pepper round the outside and pile the grapes in the centre. Pour the dressing over and serve.

Winter Root Salad

Serves 4

Winter root vegetables are normally cooked, but they make excellent salads and served in this way they retain all their nutrients and flavour.

½ celeriac, scrubbed and grated
4 medium carrots, scrubbed and grated
1 parsnip, scrubbed and grated

¼ swede, scrubbed and grated
2 small beetroots, scrubbed and grated
vinaigrette dressing (see p. 88)

If the celeriac is not to be used immediately, store it in water with a squeeze of lemon juice. Mix all the ingredients together in a salad bowl, toss in the dressing and serve.

Butterbean Salad

Serves 2–4

This is good as a starter. Other cooked beans may be substituted for the butterbeans.

4 oz (100g) butterbeans, soaked, cooked and drained
1 tablespoon onion, grated
2 tablespoons chopped parsley
¼ pint (150 ml) vinaigrette dressing (see p. 88)

½ small lettuce
1 bunch watercress, washed, yellowed leaves discarded
2 medium tomatoes, sliced

Mix the beans, onion, parsley and vinaigrette together and arrange the salad on a bed of lettuce and watercress. Top with sliced tomatoes and serve.

Pineapple Coleslaw with Tofu Dressing   *Serves 4*

In this recipe the ubiquitous coleslaw is given a tropical touch. It is extra nice if you chill the pineapple first. Serve with a dip and bread for a simple meal.

2 tablespoons (30 ml) pineapple juice from tin
¼ pint (150 ml) tofu dressing (see p. 89)
½ small white cabbage, finely chopped *or* grated

1 small tin pineapple chunks *or* 6 oz (175g) fresh pineapple, cubed
1 red dessert apple, cored and chopped
3 sticks celery, chopped

Mix the pineapple juice with the tofu dressing. Toss this mixture with the cabbage, pineapple, apple and celery.

Salad Dressings

Vinaigrette Dressing   *Makes ½ pint (275 ml)*

This dressing keeps well so make up a bottle of it ahead of time.

6 fl oz (175 ml) cold-pressed olive *or* sunflower seed oil
3 fl oz (75 ml) cider vinegar
1 teaspoon honey

2 teaspoons (10 ml) soya sauce
1 clove garlic, left whole
2 twigs of rosemary

Put the olive oil in a bottle with the cider vinegar, honey and soya sauce. Put the lid on, shake well. Add the whole clove of garlic and rosemary twigs and, ideally, leave it for a couple of days before use.

Tahini and Apple Dressing   *Serves 6 or more*

This dressing may be stored in a screw-top jar in the refrigerator and will keep for up to a month.

3 tablespoons tahini
2 teaspoons (10 ml) concentrated apple juice
½ teaspoon miso
1 small clove garlic, crushed

1 small onion, chopped
sea salt to taste
water as necessary (about 3–5 fl oz or 75–150 ml)

Put all ingredients in a blender and liquidize until smooth (about 1 minute).

Tofu Dressing   *Serves 4–6*

Tofu or bean curd is nutritious and fat free. This dressing looks like mayonnaise and has a similar consistency. It is thus a good vegan substitute. Make this dressing as needed.

1 packet tofu, drained
1 tablespoon (15 ml) olive oil
1 teaspoon (5 ml) lemon juice

1 tablespoon chopped chives
1 teaspoon honey
sea salt to taste

Put all ingredients in the blender and liquidize for 1 minute or until smooth.

Apple Chutney   *Makes 3 lb (1·4 kg)*

1 lb (450g) onions, finely chopped
½ pint (275 ml) cider vinegar
2 lb (900g) apples, cored and finely chopped
4 oz (100g) sultanas

1 teaspoon pickling spice (tied in a piece of muslin)
1 teaspoon ground ginger
1 teaspoon sea salt
12 oz (350g) raw sugar

Put the onions into a saucepan with 3 fl oz (75 ml) of the vinegar and simmer until nearly soft. Add the apples, sultanas, pickling spice, ginger, salt and a little more vinegar to stop the mixture from burning. Cook gently for about 7 minutes or until the fruit is soft, stirring occasionally. Add the remainder of the vinegar and stir in the sugar. Boil steadily without a lid until the chutney is thick (about 20 minutes). Remove pickling spices and pour the chutney into hot jars. Cover with waxed circles and cellophane.

Note: If using metal lids for the jars do not let them touch the chutney or the lids will rust and taint the chutney.

apple blossom

Breads, Pastries, Cakes and Biscuits

The grain family provides the vegan with a rich source of protein and other nutrients and the preparation of baked goods is a very satisfying way of cooking grains. There is nothing to beat making your own bread, pastries and cakes using good wholemeal flour and other unrefined ingredients. Both family and friends appreciate them and the only problem is making enough! There is no real difference between vegan baked goods and the regular variety except that we always use vegetable margarines and, more particularly, those varieties that contain no milk whey. Here we have given excellent basic recipes for wholemeal bread, sourdough bread and rye bread, together with recipes for chapattis and pitta bread. They are followed by basic pastry recipes. Also included are recipes for croissants, sweet breads, large cakes, buns, biscuits and small cakes.

Breads and Pastries

Wholemeal Bread

Makes 3 large loaves

This is a straightforward recipe that produces very good bread. If you are in a hurry you may reduce the dough proving time by half by using vitamin C to accelerate the proving process.

3 lb (1.5 kg) wholemeal bread
   flour
2 tablespoons soya flour
1 tablespoon honey *or* sugar
1 teaspoon salt
2 tablespoons (30 ml) vegetable oil

2 oz (50g) fresh yeast *or* 2
   tablespoons dried yeast
1¾ pts (1 litre) warm water
50 mg vitamin C, crushed
   (optional)

Mix the flours together with the honey (sugar) and salt, then rub in the oil. Dissolve the yeast in half the water and the vitamin C (if using it) in the other half. Combine the flour mixtures and the two volumes of liquid and mix them into the dough. Knead well. If using vitamin C put the dough straight into three greased 1 lb (450g) bread tins and miss the first proving stage. If not, prove the dough in a warm place in a covered bowl for about 1 hour or until doubled in size, then knock the dough back and pack it into the three bread tins. Preheat the oven to 425°F (220°C, gas mark 7). Prove the bread in the tins in a warm place until the dough reaches the top of the tins and then bake for 40 minutes in the hot oven. Turn the bread out and leave it to cool resting on its side on a wire rack.

Sourdough Bread   *Makes 3 long loaves*

This is a quick and easy sourdough method using wheat and rye flours. Use more wheat flour if you find the dough too sticky.

1 lb (450g) rye flour	1 pint (0.5 litre) warm water
1½ lb (700g) strong wholewheat flour	¾ oz (20g) fresh yeast *or* 2 teaspoons dried yeast
¾ oz (20g) salt	2 tablespoons caraway seeds

Weigh half the flours and salt into a bowl, mix well and then mix in half the warm water. Leave this to stand, covered, for 12–16 hours or until it smells slightly sour. Combine this with the rest of the flours, salt, yeast and water. Mix well and knead for 5 minutes. Leave the dough to prove for 1½ hours in a warm place in a covered bowl. Knock it back and, whilst doing so, knead in the caraway seeds. Shape the dough into three long loaves. Place the loaves on greased baking trays and prove for another hour, covered and in a warm place. Preheat the oven to 400°F (200°C, gas mark 6). Bake the bread in the hot oven for 1 hour. If the bread starts to brown too much at this temperature reduce it accordingly. Once baked, remove the bread from the oven and cool on a wire rack.

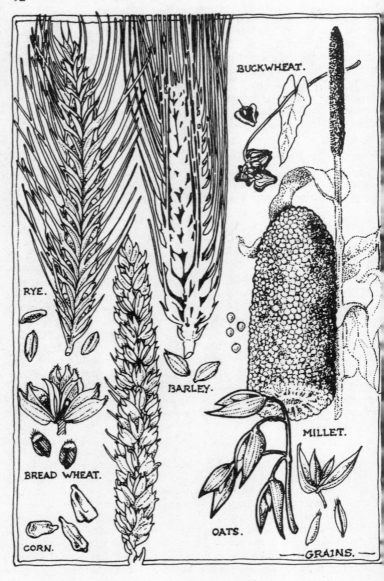

RYE.

BUCKWHEAT.

BARLEY.

BREAD WHEAT.

CORN.

MILLET.

OATS.

GRAINS.

Rye Bread   *Makes 3 long loaves*

Rye flour contains less gluten than wheat flour and, consequently,
rises less. Rye bread is heavier and more filling than yeasted wheat-
flour bread.

2 lb 4 oz (1 kg) wholemeal flour
12 oz (350g) rye flour
1 teaspoon salt
2 tablespoons (30 ml) vegetable oil
2 oz (50g) fresh yeast *or* 2
    tablespoons dried yeast

1 teaspoon honey *or* molasses
1½–1¾ pints (0.8–1 litre) warm
    water
2 tablespoons caraway seeds

In a large bowl mix the wholemeal and rye flours together with the
salt, then rub in the oil. Dissolve the yeast and honey (molasses) in the
water. Combine the flours and liquid, mix into a dough and knead
well. Prove the dough in a warm place in a covered bowl for about 1
hour (or until doubled in size), then knock it back, shape it into three
oval-shaped loaves and put them on greased baking trays. Prove again
in a warm place, covered, until the dough doubles in size for 1 hour.
Preheat oven to 425°F (220°C, gas mark 7). Bake the bread in the oven
for 40 minutes, then remove and allow to cool on a wire rack.

If you wish to speed up the baking time in this recipe add 50 mg
vitamin C to the water with the yeast and make the dough straight into
loaves for the final proving.

Chapattis   *Makes about 20*

This Indian unleavened bread is normally eaten with curries. It can be
served as an alternative, or in addition, to rice.

1 lb (450g) wholemeal flour
1 teaspoon salt

1 oz (25g) vegetable margarine
    plus 1 oz (25g) margarine, melted
About ½ pint (275 ml) cold water

Combine the flour and salt and rub in the unmelted margarine. Stir in
the water and knead well. Break 1 in (2.5 cm) lumps off the dough
and roll them with a rolling pin into 6 in (15 cm) rounds. Using a
small frying pan, dry, over a medium flame, put in a round of dough
and turn immediately it begins to look transparent. Continue to cook
until the chapatti is beginning to brown, then remove the pan from the
heat. Take the chapatti out of the pan and hold it over a high flame in
your fingertips, making sure the non-browned side is on the flame.
When it is puffed up (only a few seconds) put the chapatti on a plate
and brush it with the melted margarine. Repeat for each of the dough
rounds. Stack the cooked chapattis one on top of another. Cover with
a warm dry cloth to keep them warm.

Pitta Bread

Makes 4–6 breads

Pitta bread is a soft-textured, flat, slightly leavened bread. It is baked for a short time at a very high temperature; this produces a characteristic hollow in the middle of the bread. Pitta bread is good with dips, rice dishes, salads and deep-fried foods. Cut in half and stuffed they make excellent snack or picnic dishes.

1 lb (450g) wholemeal flour
½ teaspoon salt
1 tablespoon (15 ml) vegetable oil
½ oz (15g) fresh yeast *or* ¼ oz (10g) dried yeast

½ teaspoon honey *or* molasses
½ pint (275 ml) warm water

Mix the flour and salt together. Rub in the oil. Dissolve the yeast and honey (molasses) in the water. Combine the flour and water mixtures and mix them into a dough. Leave the dough to prove for 2 hours, covered, in a warm place. Knock the dough back and then break off lumps the size of a large potato. Roll these into oval pitta shapes about ¼ in (5 mm) thick. Leave the dough ovals in a warm place, between two floured teacloths, to rise again for another 30 minutes. Preheat the oven to 450°F (250°C, gas mark 8) and heat up two or three greased baking trays. When the pitta breads have risen, place them on the hot baking trays, sprinkle them with a little cold water and bake for about 10 minutes in the hot oven. Allow the pitta bread to cool and then either eat them straightaway or deep freeze them and reheat (5 minutes in a hot oven) for later use.

Crunchy Oat and Rye Bread   *Makes 4 × 1 lb (450g) loaves*

This is a tasty and filling bread containing three types of flour. The bran contained in oats is currently popular with nutritionists because of its beneficial effects on the digestive system.

2 oz (50g) fresh yeast *or* 1 oz (25g) dried yeast
1 tablespoon honey *or* molasses
¾ pint (450 ml) soya milk diluted with ¾ pint (450 ml) water and warmed

1½ lb (700g) wholemeal flour
6 oz (175g) medium oatmeal
6 oz (175g) coarse oatmeal
6 oz (175g) rye flour
1 tablespoon sea salt
2 tablespoons (30 ml) vegetable oil

Dissolve the yeast and honey (molasses) in the warm soya-milk solution. Mix the wholemeal flour, oatmeals, rye flour and salt in a mixing bowl. Rub in the oil and then pour in the soya-milk solution and mix well to form a sticky dough. Leave the dough to rise, covered, in a warm place for 40 minutes or until doubled in size.

Knock the dough back and divide it between four greased 1 lb (450g) loaf tins. Leave it to prove in a warm place until the dough reaches the top of the tins and then bake the bread for 40 minutes at 400°F (200°C, gas mark 6), reducing the temperature halfway to 375°F (190°C, gas mark 5). Turn the bread out and leave it to cool, wrapped in tea towels to trap the steam.

Croissants   *Makes approximately twelve*

Croissants are delicious but they contain far too much fat to be considered a regular part of a healthy diet so save them for a special celebration breakfast.

½ oz (15g) fresh yeast *or* 1½
   teaspoons dried yeast
1 oz (25g) sugar
about 7 fl oz (200 ml) soya milk
   diluted with 7 fl oz (200 ml)
   water

1 lb 2 oz (500g) wholemeal flour
2 teaspoons salt
8 oz (225g) hard vegetable
   margarine

Dissolve the yeast and sugar in 12 fl oz (350 ml) of the soya-milk solution and mix in 6 oz (175g) flour. Add the rest of the flour and salt and mix to a dough. Rest the dough, covered, for 30 minutes then roll it out ½ in (1 cm) thick into a rectangle twice as long as wide. Dot half the surface with all the margarine and fold the other half on top. Roll this out then refold and roll out again. Repeat twice more, turning the dough through 45 degrees each time. Rest the dough for 15 minutes then roll it out into a sheet ⅛ in (2·5 mm) thick. Cut the dough into strips 8 in (20 cm) wide. Cut the strips into triangles of 6 in (15 cm) base and 4 in (10 cm) sides and roll these up into a croissant shape, starting with the long side. Place the croissants on a warmed, greased baking tray and brush them with soya-milk solution. Prove them for about 30 minutes, covered, in a warm place, then brush them again with the soya-milk solution. Preheat the oven to 425°F (220°C, gas mark 7). Bake the croissants in the hot oven for 20 minutes. Remove and allow to cool. These croissants will deep freeze successfully, either baked or unbaked.

Savoury Straws   *Makes 8 oz (225g)*

These straws are good as a snack on their own or served with drinks as an appetizer.

4 oz (100g) wholemeal flour
½ teaspoon celery salt
1½ oz (40g) hard vegetable
  margarine

2 teaspoons yeast extract
2–3 fl oz (50–75 ml) hot water

Preheat oven to 450°F (230°C, gas mark 8). Combine the flour and salt and rub in the margarine. Dissolve the yeast extract in the water. Add this to the flour and mix to a stiff dough. Roll out the dough to ¾ in (2 cm) thick and cut it into strips about 4 × 1 in (10 × 2·5 cm) wide. Place the pastry strips on a greased baking tray and bake them for 10 minutes in the hot oven. Remove from the oven, loosen them from the baking sheet and allow to cool on a wire rack. Store unused straws in an airtight container.

Shortcrust Pastry   *Makes 14 oz (400g)*

7 oz (200g) wholemeal flour
1 oz (25g) soya flour

4 oz (100g) vegetable margarine
2–3 fl oz (50–75 ml) cold water

Mix the wholemeal and soya flours together. Rub in the margarine and mix in the water. Cover with a damp cloth and chill before rolling.

Note: If you like your pastry very light add 1 teaspoon baking powder to each 4 oz (100g) flour.

Puff Pastry   *Makes 1 lb (450g)*

7 oz (200g) wholemeal flour
7 oz (200g) hard vegetable
  margarine from the fridge

2 teaspoons (10 ml) lemon juice
2½ fl oz (75 ml) cold water

Sieve the flour and then add any separated bran back to the flour. Rub in 2 oz (50g) of the margarine, add the lemon juice and work in the water slowly. Roll out the rest of the margarine into a thin oblong shape on a lightly floured board, then roll out the dough to an oblong, twice as long as the margarine. Brush a little water along the edges of the pastry. Place the margarine on top of one half of the pastry, fold the other half over and seal the edges with a rolling pin. Cover and refrigerate for 15 minutes until the margarine hardens. Remove and roll to an oblong. Fold one third to the middle and the other third on top of that to make three layers. Turn the pastry one turn and roll the other way; repeat the folding process. Cover and leave for 15 minutes in the fridge. Repeat this rolling and folding procedure another two times. Leave the pastry, covered, to rest until ready to use.

Flaky Pastry   *Makes 1 lb (450g)*

7 oz (200g) wholemeal flour
4 oz (100g) hard vegetable
  margarine at room temperature

1 teaspoon (5 ml) lemon juice
¼ pint (150 ml) cold water

Sieve the flour and add any separated bran back to the flour. Rub in 1 oz (25g) of the margarine. Add the lemon juice and water and mix to a soft dough. Roll the dough out into an oblong shape, ½ in (1 cm) thick. Using another 1 oz (25g) margarine, dot knobs of margarine over two thirds of the pastry. Fold one third over then the other third on top of that. Use the rolling pin to seal the edges. Turn the dough one turn to the left, roll it into a ½ in (1 cm) thick oblong again and then repeat the dotting-with-margarine-and-folding process. Cover and rest the pastry in the fridge for 10 minutes. Repeat the rolling, dotting and folding procedure three more times, the last time without any addition of margarine. Leave the pastry covered in the fridge until ready for use.

Sweet Breads and Cakes

Walnut and Currant Bread   *Makes 2 × 1 lb (450g) loaves*

2 oz (50g) fresh yeast *or* 2
  tablespoons dried yeast
½ pint (275 ml) warm water
3 oz (75g) soft vegetable margarine
1 lb (450g) wholemeal flour

2 oz (50g) soya flour
2 oz (50g) soft brown sugar
½ teaspoon salt
2 oz (50g) walnuts
2 oz (50g) currants

Dissolve the yeast in the water. Rub the margarine into the combined wholemeal and soya flours, mix in the sugar and salt and then pour in the yeast and water. Beat the mixture into a soft dough and then leave it, covered, in a warm place to prove for about 1 hour or until doubled in size. Knock the dough back and work in the walnuts and currants. Divide the dough into two and place each half in 1 lb (450g) greased loaf tins. Cover the tins and prove in a warm place until the dough reaches the top of the tins. Preheat the oven to 425°F (220°C, gas mark 7). Bake the bread for 30 minutes, turning the tins around once. Remove the baked bread from the tins and leave to cool on a wire rack.

Muesli Tea Bread   *Makes 2 × 1 lb (450g) loaves*

1 oz (25g) fresh yeast *or* 3
  teaspoons dried yeast
1 teaspoon molasses *or* honey
6 fl oz (175 ml) soya milk diluted
  with 6 fl oz (175 ml) water,
  warmed

1 lb (450g) wholemeal flour
5 oz (150g) sugar-free muesli
1 teaspoon sea salt
2 oz (50g) soft vegetable margarine

Dissolve the yeast, molasses (honey) in the soya-milk solution.
Combine the flour, muesli and salt in a warm bowl. Rub in the
margarine and add the soya-milk mixture. Knead and leave to prove,
covered, in a warm place for 40 minutes or until doubled in size.
Knock the dough back, divide it between two 1 lb (450g) greased loaf
tins. Cover and prove in a warm place until the dough reaches the top
of the tins (30–40 minutes). Preheat the oven to 400°F (200°C, gas
mark 6). Bake for 25–30 minutes. Remove the baked bread from the
tins and leave to cool on a wire rack.

Orange Nut Bread   *Makes 2 lb (900g) loaf*

2 teaspoons dried yeast
1 teaspoon molasses dissolved in
  2 fl oz (50 ml) warm water
grated rind and juice of 1 large
  orange
1 teaspoon honey in 2 fl oz (50 ml)
  water
5 oz (150g) tofu
2 oz (50g) malt extract

8 oz (225g) wholemeal flour
1 oz (25g) soya flour
3 oz (75g) chopped hazelnuts
1 oz (25g) chopped dried banana
2 tablespoons vegetable oil
1½ fl oz (35 ml) soya milk diluted
  with 1½ fl oz (35 ml) water
1 tablespoon (15 ml) concentrated
  apple juice

Stir the yeast into the molasses and water solution and set aside. In a
small pan cook the orange rind, orange juice and honey and water over
a low heat for 10 minutes. Mix the tofu with the malt extract and fold
the mixture into the flours, hazelnuts, banana and oil. Stir into this
mixture the soya-milk solution, apple juice, yeast solution and
orange-juice mixture to form a firm dough. Add more orange juice if
the dough is too stiff. Put the dough into a greased 2 lb (900g) loaf tin
and leave it to prove, covered, in a warm place for 1 hour or until
doubled in size. Preheat the oven to 350°F (180°C, gas mark 4). Bake
the bread for 35–40 minutes. Remove the baked bread from the tin and
leave to cool on a wire grill.

Carrot and Banana Bread
Makes 2 lb (900g) loaf

9 oz (250g) wholemeal flour
1 oz (25g) soya flour
3 teaspoons baking power
1 teaspoon mixed spice
4 oz (100g) soft vegetable
  margarine

2 oz (50g) soft brown sugar
3 fl oz (75 ml) cold water
4 oz (100g) mashed banana
4 oz (100g) grated carrot
1 oz (25g) sesame seeds

Preheat oven to 350°F (180°C, gas mark 4). Sieve together the flours, baking powder and mixed spice. Add any separated bran back to the mixture. Cream the margarine and sugar together. Stir into this the water, banana and carrot and fold this mixture into the sieved flour. Beat together and then place the mixture into a greased 2 lb (900g) loaf tin. Sprinkle the sesame seeds on top. Bake for about 1 hour in the oven. Remove the baked bread from the tin and leave it to cool on a wire rack.

Banana and Date Loaf
Makes 2 lb (900g) loaf

7 oz (200g) wholemeal flour
1 oz (25g) soya flour
3 teaspoons baking powder
1 teaspoon mixed spice
4 oz (100g) soft vegetable
  margarine

2 oz (50g) Muscavado sugar
2 teaspoons honey
2 bananas, mashed
2 oz (50g) chopped dates
3 fl oz (75 ml) water

Preheat oven to 350°F (180°C, gas mark 4). Sieve together the flours, baking powder and mixed spice, returning any separated bran back into the flours. Cream the margarine, sugar and honey together. Add to this the banana, dates, sieved flour and water. Beat the mixture into a smooth dough and then put it into a greased 2 lb (900g) loaf tin. Bake for 1–1½ hours in the preheated oven. The loaf is baked when a skewer stuck into it comes out clean. Remove the baked loaf from the tin and leave it to cool on a wire rack.

Banana Bread

Makes 1 lb (450g) loaf

2 oz (50g) margarine, melted
2 oz (50g) Barbados sugar
6 oz (175g) wholemeal flour
2 teaspoons baking powder
2 bananas, mashed

1 teaspoon (5 ml) natural vanilla extract
1½ fl oz (35 ml) soya milk diluted with 1½ fl oz (35 ml) water

Preheat oven to 350°F (180°C, gas mark 4). Cream together the margarine and sugar until light and fluffy. Sieve the flour with the baking powder. Add this with the bananas, vanilla and soya-milk solution to the creamed margarine and beat together. Pack the mixture into a greased 1 lb (450g) loaf tin and bake in the preheated oven for 1 hour. Remove the baked loaf from the tin and leave to cool on a wire rack.

Hazelnut, Orange and Banana Cake

Makes 9 in (23 cm) cake

5 oz (150g) wholemeal flour
2 teaspoons baking powder
8 oz (225g) soft vegetable margarine
4 oz (100g) Barbados sugar
4 oz (100g) hazelnuts, roasted and ground *or* crushed

8 oz (225g) dried bananas
juice and grated rind of 1 large orange
½ teaspoon ground cinnamon

Preheat oven to 350°F (180°C, gas mark 4). Sieve together the flour and baking powder. Cream the margarine and sugar together for about 5 minutes or until light and fluffy. Fold into this the flour and baking powder and stir in the ground hazelnuts. Place half this cake mixture into a greased, lined 9 in (23 cm) cake tin. Put the dried bananas through a mincer or finely chop them in a blender or processor. Add the orange juice, rind and cinnamon to the bananas and mix well. Spread this mixture evenly over the cake batter in the tin. Place the remaining half of the cake batter on top and smooth over. Bake for 1–1½ hours in the preheated oven. The cake is baked when a skewer stuck into it comes out clean. Remove the baked cake from the tin and leave to cool on a wire rack.

Tofu Apple 'Cheesecake' *Makes 8 in (20 cm) cake*

Tofu or bean curd is made from soya beans. It contains no fat, is nutritious and soft in texture. It can be used in many of the ways cheese is used – as it is in this vegan cheesecake.

7 oz (200g) wholemeal flour
1 oz (25g) soya flour
2 teaspoons ground cinnamon
2 oz (50g) soft margarine
6 fl oz (175 ml) water
2 oz (50g) dates, chopped
3 tablespoons (45 ml) lemon juice

11 oz (300g) tofu
½ teaspoon grated lemon rind
3 tablespoons (45 ml) concentrated apple juice
sugar-free blackcurrant jam for topping

Preheat oven to 350°F (180°C, gas mark 4). Mix together in a large bowl the flours and cinnamon. Rub in the margarine and add about 4 fl oz (100 ml) water to mix to a softish pastry. Roll the pastry out and line a greased 8 in (20 cm) sandwich tin with it (the base only). Prick the pastry lining with a fork and then bake it for 10 minutes in preheated oven. Simmer the dates in 2 fl oz (50 ml) water and the lemon juice for 5 minutes. Put the dates and liquid into a blender with the tofu, lemon rind and apple juice. Liquidize for 1 minute or until smooth. Pour this mixture into the pie shell and bake for about 20 minutes in the preheated oven or until the filling is set. Take the cake from the oven, remove it from the tin and top with a thin spreading of sugar-free blackcurrant jam.

Apple Cake *Makes 8 in (20 cm) cake*

4 oz (100g) soft vegetable margarine
3 oz (75g) Barbados sugar
2 dessert apples, cored and grated
8 oz (225g) wholemeal flour
1 tablespoon soya flour
1 tablespoon wheatgerm

3 teaspoons ground cinnamon
3 teaspoons baking power
2 oz (50g) sultanas
2 tablespoons (30 ml) soya milk
juice of ½ lemon
water if necessary

Preheat oven to 375°F (190°C, gas mark 5). Cream the margarine and sugar together for 5 minutes or until light and fluffy. Stir in the apples. Mix together the flours, wheatgerm, cinnamon, baking powder and sultanas. Stir this into the creamed margarine and apples and add the soya milk and lemon juice plus a little water if the batter is too thick. Pour the batter into a greased 8 in (20 cm) sandwich tin, with a piece of greaseproof paper in the base. Bake for 40 minutes to 1 hour in the preheated oven. The cake is baked when a skewer stuck into it comes out clean. Release the cake from the tin and allow to cool on a wire rack.

Fruit Cake _Makes 1¼ lb (550g) cake_

8 oz (225g) wholemeal flour
1 oz (25g) soya flour
2 oz (50g) Barbados sugar
4 oz (100g) soft vegetable
  margarine
4 oz (100g) dried fruit
1 level teaspoon agar agar

grated rind of ½ lemon
1 oz (25g) roughly chopped
  walnuts
2 level teaspoons baking powder
1 level teaspoon mixed spice
½ level teaspoon ground cinnamon
water to mix

Preheat oven to 325°F (170°C, gas mark 3). Combine the flours. Cream together the sugar and margarine until light and fluffy. Stir the dried fruit into the flour (this helps to prevent the fruit sinking in the baked cake) and then mix the fruit and flour into the creamed margarine. Dissolve the agar agar in a little water and mix this in as well. Add the lemon rind, walnuts, baking powder, mixed spice and cinnamon and mix well. Now add a little water spoon by spoon until the batter has a soft dropping consistency. Line the bottom of a 1 lb (450g) bread tin with greaseproof paper. Pour in the cake mixture and bake in the preheated oven for 40 minutes. Remove the cake from the tin and allow to cool on a wire rack.

Carrot and Orange Cake _Makes 6 in (15 cm) cake_

4 oz (100g) soft vegetable
  margarine
3 oz (75g) Barbados sugar
4 oz (100g) finely grated carrot
grated rind of 1 orange
8 oz (225g) 100 or 85 per cent self-
  raising flour

1 level teaspoon baking powder
2 level teaspoons ground cinnamon

Topping
2 oz (50g) creamed coconut
juice of 1 orange _or_ 2 fl oz (50 ml)
  orange juice

Preheat oven to 350°F (180°C, gas mark 4). Cream the margarine with the sugar until light and fluffy. Stir in the carrot and orange rind. Fold in the flour, baking powder and cinnamon. Transfer the mixture to a greased 6 in (15 cm) cake tin with a circle of greaseproof paper in the base. Bake for 1 hour in the preheated oven. Release the cake from the tin and set it to cool on a wire rack. Meanwhile, melt the coconut over a low heat. Stir in the orange juice and spread the mixture evenly over the cake.

Buns, Biscuits and Small Cakes

Hot Cross Buns
Makes 15 buns

1 lb 2 oz (500g) wholemeal flour
2 oz (50g) soya flour
1 teaspoon cinnamon
1 teaspoon mixed spice
2 oz (50g) soft vegetable margarine
1 oz (25g) fresh yeast *or* 1½ teaspoons dried yeast
25 mg vitamin C tablet, crushed
4½ fl oz (125 ml) soya milk diluted with 4½ fl oz (125 ml) water, warmed

2 tablespoons clear honey
3 oz (75g) sultanas
3 oz (75g) currants
2 oz (50g) raisins
pastry trimmings for crosses
1 tablespoon (15 ml) boiling water

Combine the flours, cinnamon and mixed spice and rub in the margarine. Dissolve the yeast and vitamin C in the warm soya-milk solution and stir in half the honey. Pour this soya-milk solution into the flour mixture and mix together to form a soft dough. Add a little more wholemeal flour if the dough is too soft. Knead the dough well, cover and leave for 10 minutes. Work in the sultanas, currants and raisins and then divide the dough into 15 portions. Roll them into balls and place these on greased baking trays. Cover and leave in a warm place for 1½ hours or until doubled in size. Preheat oven to 450°F (230°C, gas mark 8). Roll the pastry trimmings into long strips, cut them up and make crosses on the buns. Bake the buns in the preheated oven for 15 minutes or until nicely browned, turning the trays once. Remove the buns from the oven and throw away the pastry crosses. Dissolve the remaining honey in the boiling water and brush the hot buns with it. Remove the buns from the baking trays and leave them to cool on a wire rack.

Oatbran and Oatgerm Scones
Makes 8 scones

As well as being delicious, oatbran is a useful dietary fibre. Oatbran is also reputed to help in the lowering of high blood pressure.

4 oz (100g) wholemeal flour
2 teaspoons baking powder
½ teaspoon mixed spice
4 oz (100g) oatbran and oatgerm mixture

1½ oz (40g) soft vegetable margarine
2 oz (50g) sultanas
1½ fl oz (35 ml) soya milk diluted with 1½ fl oz (35 ml) water

Preheat oven to 425°F (220°C, gas mark 7). Sieve the flour with the baking powder and mixed spice, returning any separated bran back into the mixture. Add the oatbran and oatgerm, mix them well and then rub in the margarine. Stir in the sultanas, then the soya–milk solution and mix to a soft dough. Roll the dough out on a floured board to ¾ in (2 cm) thick and cut out dough circles with a 2 in (5 cm) fluted cutter. Place the dough circles on a greased baking tray and bake in the preheated oven for about 15 minutes. Remove the trays from the oven, transfer the scones to a wire grill and leave to cool.

Oatcakes   *Makes about 20 cakes*

8 oz (225g) medium oatmeal
2 oz (50g) wholemeal flour
1 teaspoon baking powder

2 oz (50g) soft vegetable margarine
boiling water to mix

Preheat oven to 375°F (190°C, gas mark 5). Mix together the oatmeal, flour and baking powder. Rub in the margarine and add just enough boiling water to form a firm dough. Knead the dough well and roll it out to ⅛ in (3 mm) thick. Cut the oatcakes out with a plain 2½ in (6 cm) cutter. Place them on a greased baking tray and bake for 10 minutes in the preheated oven. Remove the tray from the oven, transfer the biscuits to a wire grill and cool. Store unused oatcakes in an airtight container.

Apple and Oat Muffins   *Makes about 16 muffins*

4 oz (100g) porridge oats
11 fl oz (350 ml) water
2 tablespoons (30 ml) vegetable oil
1 tablespoon molasses
3 oz (75g) sultanas

1 dessert apple, cored and grated
2 oz (50g) wholemeal flour
1 tablespoon soya flour
2 teaspoons baking powder

Preheat oven to 375°F (190°C, gas mark 5). Put the oats and water in a saucepan and cook until the mixture thickens (about 5 minutes). Remove the pan from the heat and stir in the oil, molasses, sultanas and grated apple. Sieve the flours and baking powder together, returning any bran that separates. Stir the contents of the pan into the flour mixture and mix well together. Divide the mixture between about sixteen muffin tins or paper cases or greased bun tins. Bake for 25 minutes in the preheated oven. Remove the muffins from their containers and leave to cool on a wire rack.

Honey and Malt Flapjacks   *Makes 10 flapjacks*

3 oz (75g) vegetable margarine   1 oz (25g) malt extract
4 oz (100g) clear honey   8 oz (225g) porridge oats

Preheat oven to 400°F (200°C, gas mark 6). Heat the margarine, honey
and malt extract in a large saucepan over a low heat. When the
margarine has melted, stir in the oats and mix well. Press the mixture
into a greased baking tin about 8 × 6 in (20 × 15 cm). Smooth the
surface (a child's rolling pin, dipped in hot water, is good for this).
Bake for 20–25 minutes in the preheated oven. Turn the biscuit out of
the tin and cut into ten pieces. Leave to cool on a wire rack.

Hazelnut Shortcake   *Makes 6 pieces*

4 oz (100g) soft vegetable margarine   2 oz (50g) hazelnuts, roasted and
2 oz (50g) wholemeal flour   coarsely chopped
2 oz (50g) Barbados sugar

Preheat oven to 375°F (190°C, gas mark 5). Melt the margarine in a
saucepan over a low heat. Stir in the rest of the ingredients and press
the mixture into a small (about 6 in (15 cm) square) greased tin. Bake
for about 25 minutes in the preheated oven. Cut the shortcake into six
pieces immediately, but do not remove them from the tin until cool.

Coconut and Oat Biscuits   *Makes 18 biscuits*

4 oz (100g) soft vegetable   1 oz (25g) desiccated coconut
  margarine   5 oz (150g) porridge oats
2 oz (50g) Barbados sugar   1 tablespoon wheatgerm
1 teaspoon (5 ml) natural vanilla   1 tablespoon sesame seeds
  essence   1 oz (25g) raisins, chopped

Preheat oven to 375°F (190°C, gas mark 5). Cream the margarine and
the sugar until light and fluffy (about 5 minutes). Mix in the vanilla
essence, coconut, oats, wheatgerm, sesame seeds and chopped raisins.
Place dessertspoonfuls of the mixture onto a greased baking sheet and
bake for 15 minutes in the preheated oven. Remove the baking sheet
from the oven, loosen the biscuits and allow them to cool on a wire
rack.

Carob Oat Crunchies
Makes about 20 crunchies

4 oz (100g) wholemeal flour
4 oz (100g) rolled oats
½ teaspoon baking powder
4 oz (100g) soft vegetable
  margarine
1 tablespoon honey

2 oz (50g) hazelnuts, roasted and
  roughly chopped
1½ tablespoons (25 ml) of soya
  milk diluted with 1½ tablespoons
  (25 ml) water
4 oz (100g) plain carob bar

Preheat oven to 400°F (200°C, gas mark 6). Mix together the flour, oats and baking powder. Rub in the margarine and honey. Mix in the hazelnuts and soya-milk solution. Form the mixture into small balls about 1 in (2·5 cm) in diameter and place them on a greased baking tray. Flatten the balls to form small rounds about ½ in (14 mm) thick. Bake for 20 minutes in the preheated oven. Cool the crunchies on a wire rack. Melt the carob bar in a bowl over a pan of simmering water. Brush the underside of each crunchy with the carob and leave them upside down to cool.

Date and Lemon Slices
Makes 10 slices

6 oz (175g) shortcrust pastry (see
  p. 96)
12 oz (350g) dates, chopped

grated rind of 1 lemon
5 fl oz (150 ml) water

Preheat oven to 350°F (180°C, gas mark 4). Roll out half the pastry and press it into the bottom of a Swiss-roll tin. Roll out the rest of the pastry for the top. Simmer the dates and lemon rind in the water, covered, for about 10 minutes, or until the dates are soft. Allow this mixture to cool then spread it over the pastry in the tin. Cover with the top pastry, press the edges together, prick the top with a fork and bake for 20 minutes in the preheated oven. Cut the cake into slices while still hot and then allow to cool.

Date and Oat Slices
Makes 12 slices

The sugar in this recipe is optional but, if it is left in, it helps to wean a child off commercial cakes and biscuits.

6 oz (175g) soft vegetable
  margarine
1 oz (25g) soft brown sugar,
  optional
8 oz (225g) wholemeal flour
1 level teaspoon ground cinnamon

½ teaspoon baking powder
4 oz (100g) rolled oats
8 oz (225g) dates
5 fl oz (150 ml) water
juice of ½ lemon

Preheat oven to 400°F (200°C, gas mark 6). Cream the margarine with the sugar. Sift the flour, cinnamon and baking powder together. Return any separated bran to the mix and then add the oats. Rub in the margarine and sugar mixture. Simmer the dates in the water and lemon juice for 5 minutes. Spread half the margarine-and-flour mixture in the bottom of a swiss-roll tin. Cover with the date mixture and top it with the rest of the margarine-and-flour mixture. Bake for 20–25 minutes in the preheated oven. Remove the tin from the oven, cut the cake into slices and then allow to cool.

Coconut and Orange Cakes   *Makes 12 cakes*

6 oz (175g) soft vegetable
  margarine
1 oz (25g) Barbados sugar,
  optional
6 oz (175g) wholemeal flour
1 oz (25g) soya flour

3 oz (75g) desiccated coconut
2 teaspoons ground cinnamon
2 teaspoons baking powder
2 oz (50g) trail mix *or* 1 oz (25g)
  each of peanuts and sultanas
8 fl oz (225 ml) orange juice

Preheat the oven to 350°F (180°C, gas mark 4). Cream the margarine with the sugar for 5 minutes until light and fluffy. Mix into this the flours, coconut, cinnamon, baking powder and trail mix or alternative. Lastly add the orange juice and mix well. Put the mixture into a greased 10 × 8 in (25 × 16 cm) tin and bake for 40 minutes in the preheated oven. Cut the cake into twelve squares whilst still hot, and then allow to cool before removing the cakes from the tin.

Easter Biscuits   *Makes about 30 biscuits*

For a nutritious snack eat these biscuits any time of year. As your tastebuds adapt to less sweetening cut down the sugar content in this recipe.

7 oz (200g) wholemeal flour
1 oz (25g) soya flour
¼ teaspoon baking powder
2 teaspoons grated lemon rind
3 oz (75g) Barbados sugar

4 oz (100g) soft vegetable
  margarine
2 oz (50g) currants
about 2 fl oz (50 ml) cold water

Preheat the oven to 425°F (220°C, gas mark 7). Sieve together the flours and baking powder, returning the bran to the mixture. Add the lemon rind and sugar. Rub in the margarine, stir in the currants and as much of the water as necessary to make a pliable dough. Roll out to ¼ in (5 mm) thick and cut out with 2 in (5 cm) fluted cutter. Place the biscuits on greased baking trays and bake for 15–20 minutes in the preheated oven. Cool on a wire rack and store in an airtight container.

Desserts

These desserts are good and delicious. They use unrefined ingredients and minimum amounts of sugar (very often none at all) and fat. You can enjoy them with a clear conscience.

Apricot Rice Pudding   *Serves 4–6*

The recipe uses dried apricots but fresh ones, when available, can be substituted. With dried apricots serve the rice pudding hot as a warming autumn or winter dessert. With fresh apricots serve the pudding chilled.

8 oz (225g) dried apricots, chopped
boiling water
2 tablespoons apricot jam
6 oz (175g) short-grain brown rice

½ pint (275 ml) soya milk diluted
    with the ½ pint (275 ml) water
½ teaspoon ground nutmeg
grated rind of 1 lemon

Place the apricots in a saucepan and cover with boiling water. Cover the pan and cook the apricots for about 40 minutes over a low heat until soft. Drain, if necessary. Stir the jam into the cooked apricots. Place the rice in a saucepan with a well-fitting lid and add the diluted soya milk, nutmeg and lemon rind and simmer over a low heat for about 40 minutes or until the rice is cooked and the soya milk absorbed. Pile the rice into the centre of a serving dish and pour the apricots over the rice.

Prune and Redcurrant Wine Jellies   *Serves 4–6*

This is a special treat to be saved for the short season in the summer when redcurrants are available fresh. If the recipe contains too much wine for your taste, reduce the amount and substitute water.

1 lb (450g) prunes
½ pint (275 ml) red wine
¼ pint (150 ml) water
rind and juice of 1 medium orange

8 oz (225g) redcurrants, topped and tailed
½ oz (15g) agar agar

Place the prunes in a saucepan with the wine, water and orange rind and bring to the boil. Lower heat and simmer, covered, for 40 minutes or until the prunes are cooked.

Place the redcurrants in another saucepan over a low heat. Cook for about 5 minutes, remove and rub them through a sieve. Soak the agar agar in the orange juice. Strain the hot liquid from the cooked prunes onto the agar agar, stirring all the time until the agar agar has dissolved. Discard the orange rind from the prunes and place the prunes in the bottom of individual glass dishes. Add the redcurrant juice to the agar agar and prune juice and leave to cool. At the point of setting pour this mixture over the prunes. Cool the jellies in the refrigerator before serving.

Steamed Fruit Pudding   *Serves 4*

Serve this pudding with a little fresh-fruit salad and undiluted soya milk. This recipe contains no fat of any kind, it is not rich like Christmas pudding and is relatively low in calories.

1 wholemeal crust of bread *or* 2 oz (50g) breadcrumbs
8 oz (225g) mixed dried fruit
½ teaspoon mixed spice
½ teaspoon ground cinnamon

grated rind of 1 lemon *or* orange
1 tablespoon soya flour
1 tablespoon roughly chopped nuts
6 fl oz (175 ml) cold water

Put all the ingredients together (except the water) and mix well. Stir in the water to make a fairly stiff mixture. Spoon this into a greased pudding basin. Cover and steam for 2½ hours, or 1½ hours in a pressure cooker.

Pumpkin Pie

Serves 4

Pumpkin pie is very popular in America but, for some reason, not well known in Britain. Do try it; it makes a nice change from the usual fruit pies.

4 oz (100g) apple, peeled, cored and chopped
8 oz (225g) pumpkin, peeled and chopped
¼ pint (150 ml) water

6 oz (175g) sultanas
1 teaspoon mixed spice
1 teaspoon grated orange rind
4 oz (100g) shortcrust pastry (p. 96)

Simmer the apple and pumpkin in the water for 15 minutes. Add the sultanas, mixed spice and orange rind and cook for a further 5 minutes. Preheat oven to 400°F (200°C, gas mark 6). Transfer the pumpkin mixture to a 9 in (23 cm) pie dish, roll out the pastry and cover the pie. Bake for 20–25 minutes in the hot oven. Serve with nut cream or soya milk (pp. 117 and 129–30).

Apricot and Apple Crumble

Serves 6

4 oz (100g) wholemeal flour
2 oz (50g) rolled oats
2 oz (50g) soft vegetable margarine
1 tablespoon sesame seeds
2 oz (50g) soft brown sugar
½ teaspoon ground cinnamon

4 oz (100g) dried apricots, chopped
1 lb (450g) cooking apples, sliced
2 oz (50g) dates, chopped
1 tablespoon (15 ml) lemon juice
½ pint (275 ml) water

Combine the flour and oats and rub in the margarine to make a crumble. Add the sesame seeds, sugar and cinnamon and mix well. Put the apricots, apples, dates, lemon juice and water into a pressure cooker or ordinary saucepan. Bring up to pressure and cook for 5 minutes, or 20 minutes in an ordinary saucepan. Transfer the mixture to a casserole dish, cover with the prepared crumble and bake for 25 minutes in a preheated oven at 400°F (200°C, gas mark 6).

Blackberry and Apple Flan

Serves 6

This flan is best with fresh blackberries but out-of-season tinned ones still give good results.

4 oz (100g) shortcrust pastry (p. 96)
1½ lb (675g) cooking apples, chopped except for 1 apple
8 oz (225g) blackberries

2 tablespoons (30 ml) water
1 teaspoon agar agar
juice of ½ lemon
1 tablespoon honey
1 tablespoon (15 ml) hot water

Roll out the pastry and line an 8 in (20 cm) flan dish. Put the chopped apples and half the blackberries in a saucepan with 2 tablespoons (30 ml) water. Cover and cook for 15 minutes on a low heat. Press the mixture through a sieve and collect the juice. Stir into this the agar agar and bring to the boil. Stir well. Pour this thickened juice into the flan case. Preheat oven to 400°F (200°C, gas mark 6). Slice the remaining apple, toss the slices in the lemon juice and decorate the flan with both them and the rest of the blackberries. Bake the flan in the hot oven for 15 minutes. Allow it to cool, mix together the honey and hot water and spoon the mixture over the flan.

Tropical Fruit Salad   *Serves 4–6*

This is quick to prepare and delicious but the ingredients can be expensive. Save this fruit salad for the occasional special meal.

½ ripe pineapple, peeled, cored and chopped
1 banana, sliced
2 kiwi fruits, peeled, halved and sliced

1 mango, peeled and chopped
1 tablespoon (15 ml) lemon juice
¼ pint (150 ml) grape juice

Mix together the pineapple, banana, kiwi fruit and mango. Pour the lemon and grape juice over the fruit and serve chilled.

Banana Rice Pudding   *Serves 8*

6 oz (175g) short-grain brown rice, washed
boiling water
1 teaspoon (5 ml) natural vanilla essence

1½ pints (900 ml) soya milk
3 dried bananas, chopped
2 oz (50g) hazelnuts, roasted and chopped

Put the rice in a greased pudding dish and just cover with boiling water. Bake for 40 minutes at 350°F (180°C, gas mark 4). Remove the dish from the oven and stir in the vanilla essence, soya milk and dried bananas. Return the dish to the oven and cook for another 40 minutes. Serve hot sprinkled with the hazelnuts.

Persimmon and Lemon Freeze

Serves 2–3

2 persimmons
2 tablespoons clear honey
juice of 1 lemon

Halve the persimmons, scoop out the pulp and put it in a blender with the honey and lemon. Liquidize for 1 minute or until smooth. Pour this mixture into a small plastic container and deep freeze it for 2–3 hours. It is then ready to be served.

Gooseberry and Orange Wheatgerm Dessert

Serves 6

3 tablespoons wheatgerm
juice of 2 oranges, grated rind of
   1 orange, segments of 1 orange
1 lb (450g) gooseberries, cooked
   and puréed with as little water as
   possible

4 tablespoons walnuts, roughly
   chopped
soya milk to serve
a little rosehip syrup

Soak the wheatgerm in the orange juice for about 1 hour. Mix in the gooseberry purée, walnuts, orange segments and orange rind. Chill the mixture and serve with soya milk and a trickle of rosehip syrup.

Tofu Ice Cream

Serves 4–6

Serve this with a hot pudding or on its own or, alternatively, make ice lollies for the children.

3 teaspoons agar agar
¼ pint (150 ml) hot water
8 oz (225g) tofu
¼ pint (150 ml) soya milk
3 tablespoons (45 ml) concentrated
   apple juice

2 teaspoons honey
2 teaspoons (10 ml) vanilla essence
2 ripe bananas, peeled

Put the hot water and agar agar into the blender and liquidize until the agar agar has dissolved. Add the other ingredients and liquidize until smooth (about 1 minute). Transfer the thick cream to a plastic container and place it in the deep freeze. After two hours give the ice cream a whisk and return it to the freezer. It is ready to eat in another hour.

Baked Apples
Serves 4

4 Bramley cooking apples, cored
3 tablespoons sultanas *or* currants
  or a mixture of both

1 tablespoon chopped walnuts
4 dates, stoned
1 tablespoon maple syrup

Preheat oven to 350°F (180°C, gas mark 4). Wash the apples and score through the skin, with the point of a sharp knife, around the circumference. Place them on a greased baking tray. Stuff them with a mixture of the sultanas (currants) and nuts. Plug each apple with a date, and cover with maple syrup. Bake for 30 minutes in the hot oven.

Sultana Tart
Serves 6

This tart is good with pumpkin custard (see p. 117).

4 oz (100g) shortcrust pastry (see
  p. 96)
12 oz (350g) sultanas, washed
½ pint (275 ml) water

grated rind of 1 lemon
1 teaspoon ground cinnamon
¼ teaspoon agar agar

Roll out pastry to line an 8 in (20 cm) flan dish. Prick and bake for 15 minutes at 350°F (180°C, gas mark 4). Put the sultanas through a mincer, then into a saucepan with the water, lemon rind and cinnamon. Bring to the boil, then cover the pan and simmer for 5 minutes. Sprinkle the agar agar over this mixture, stirring well with a wooden spoon until the mixture thickens (about 2 minutes). Pour the filling into the pastry case and serve hot or cold.

Fruit and Almond Charlotte
Serves 4–6

1½ oz (40g) soft brown sugar
5 oz (150g) wholemeal
  breadcrumbs
3 oz (75g) ground almonds
grated rind and juice of ½ lemon
1 lb (450g) cooking apples, thinly
  sliced

1½ oz (40g) raisins, washed
1 teaspoon (5 ml) natural almond
  essence
1 oz (25g) soft vegetable
  margarine

Combine the sugar, breadcrumbs, almonds and lemon rind together and mix well. Preheat oven to 350°F (180°C, gas mark 4). Make the following layers in a deep baking dish: apples, raisins, breadcrumb mixture, apples, raisins and breadcrumb mixture. Mix the lemon juice and almond essence and sprinkle over the top of the charlotte. Dot the top with knobs of margarine and bake in the hot oven, covered, for 25 minutes. Remove the cover and bake a further 15 minutes.

Strawberry Shortcake   *Makes 9 in (23 cm) cake*

6 oz (175g) wholemeal flour
1½ teaspoons baking power
1 teaspoon (5 ml) almond essence
4 oz (100g) soft vegetable
  margarine
3 oz (75g) ground almonds

1 oz (25g) soft brown sugar
4 oz (100g) strawberry jam (sugar-
  free variety if possible)
½ teaspoon agar agar
4 oz (100g) strawberries, halved

Preheat oven to 350°F (180°C, gas mark 4). Combine the flour and baking powder, add the almond essence and rub in the margarine. Work in the ground almonds and sugar. Press the mixture into a 9 in (23 cm) flan tin or dish. Bake for 30 minutes in the hot oven. Allow the shortcake to cool then remove it from the tin. Heat up the jam gently and when it is just boiling stir in the agar agar. Pour this mixture over the shortcake, decorate the top with strawberries and allow to set before serving.

Fruit Salad with Ginger   *Serves 4*

1 dessert apple, chopped
1 ripe pear, chopped
1 banana, sliced
1 peach *or* other soft fruit, chopped
1 dessertspoon chopped preserved
  ginger
1 oz (25g) raisins, washed

1 tablespoon (15 ml) concentrated
  apple juice
4 fl oz (100 ml) orange juice
1 teaspoon (5 ml) of the ginger
  syrup from the preserved ginger
  jar

Mix together in a serving bowl the apple, pear, banana, peach, ginger and raisins. Whisk the apple juice, orange juice and ginger syrup together and pour this sauce over the fruit. Chill before serving.

Fresh Currant and Dried Fruit Compote   *Serves 4*

Serve this dessert with soya milk and chopped, roasted hazelnuts sprinkled over the top.

8 prunes
2 dried bananas
4 dried apricots
1 punnet blackcurrants *or*

redcurrants, topped, tailed and
  washed
1 tablespoon molasses

Wash the prunes, bananas and apricots and put them in a saucepan. Put the black or red currants on top, and just cover with water. Cover, bring to the boil and simmer for 20 minutes. Stir in the molasses and serve hot or cold.

Prune Crème
Serves 4

6 oz (175g) prunes, soaked and
  covered in water, gently boiled
  for 20 minutes, drained (reserve
  juice)
2 tablespoons (30 ml) soya milk
3 digestive biscuits, crushed

grated rind of ½ lemon
½ teaspoon ground cinnamon
1 tablespoon roasted and ground
  hazelnuts

Remove the stones and put the prunes in a blender with the soya milk.
Liquidize for 2 minutes or until smooth. Add a little of the prune
cooking water if necessary to keep the blades turning. Add to the
blender the biscuits, the lemon rind, cinnamon and nuts. Liquidize for
1 more minute or until smooth. Transfer the crème to a serving dish
and chill.

Apricot Ice Cream
Serves 6

6 oz (175g) dried apricots, soaked,
  covered in water and gently
  boiled for 20 minutes
1 tablespoon honey

2 teaspoons (10 ml) vanilla essence
½ pint (275 ml) soya milk, diluted
  with the ½ pint (275 ml) water
2 teaspoons agar agar

Put the apricots, honey and vanilla essence into a blender. Bring the
diluted soya milk to the boil, sprinkle the agar agar over and pour this
mixture into the blender on top of the apricots. Liquidize for 2 minutes
or until smooth. Transfer the contents of the blender to a plastic
container and put it into a freezer for 2 hours. Remove and whisk the
ice cream to break up any ice crystals. Return it to the freezer; it is
ready to serve after 1 more hour.

Pear Hélène
Serves 6

6 halves of canned pear (tinned in
  juice, not syrup)

carob chocolate blancmange
  (p. 124)
a little carob chocolate, grated

Put a pear half in the bottom of each of six dessert bowls. Make the
chocolate blancmange. Pour it over the pears and allow to cool. Serve
sprinkled with grated carob chocolate.

Raspberry Sorbet

Serves 4

3 fl oz (75 ml) soya milk, diluted
 with 3 fl oz (75 ml) water
1 teaspoon agar agar

8 oz (225g) raspberries, mashed
2 tablespoons honey
1 teaspoon (5 ml) lemon juice

Bring the diluted soya milk to the boil and sprinkle the agar agar over it. Mix in the raspberries, honey and lemon juice. Transfer the mixture to a plastic container and put it into a freezer for 2 hours. Remove and whisk the sorbet to break up any ice crystals. Return it to the freezer; it is ready to serve after 1 more hour.

Apricot Dessert

Serves 4

8 oz (225g) apricots, stones
 (kernels) removed, washed

peeled rind of 1 lemon
water to cover

Put the apricots in a saucepan with the lemon rind. Cover with water and bring to the boil. Cover and simmer for 10 minutes. Take off the heat and leave to soak for a few hours before chilling and serving.

Note: If you smash the apricot kernels open you will find delicious nuts inside. Add these to the apricots in the pan for a lovely almond flavour. They are edible.

Apple and Date Sponge

Serves 6

1 lb (450g) cooking apples,
 chopped
1 banana, sliced
2 oz (50g) dates, chopped
3 fl oz (75 ml) water
4 oz (100g) soft vegetable
 margarine
3 oz (75g) soft brown sugar

4 oz (100g) hazelnuts, roasted and
 ground
5 oz (150g) wholemeal flour
1 oz (25g) soya flour
2 teaspoons baking powder
1½ fl oz (35 ml) soya milk diluted
 with 1½ fl oz (35 ml) water

Gently boil the apples, banana and dates in the water over a low heat until nearly soft or put them in a pressure cooker, bring up to pressure, turn the heat off and leave the lid on for 1 hour. Put the mixture into a greased baking dish. Preheat the oven to 350°F (180°C, gas mark 4). To make the sponge, cream the margarine and sugar together until light and fluffy. Carefully fold in the nuts, flours, baking powder and soya milk. Spoon or pipe the sponge mixture over the apple mixture and bake for 40 minutes in the hot oven.

Cashew Nut Cream

Serve this cream chilled, over fruit or cereal dishes.

4 oz (100g) cashew nuts
1 teaspoon (5 ml) natural vanilla
    extract
¼ pint (150 ml) water

Put all the ingredients into a blender and liquidize for 1–2 minutes or until smooth.

Pumpkin Custard (or Hallowe'en Custard!)

2 lb (900g) pumpkin, deseeded and   1 tablespoon honey
    cut into 1 in (2.5 cm) cubes   1 tablespoon raw sugar (optional)
¼ pint (150 ml) water   1 tablespoon arrowroot
1 teaspoon (5 ml) natural vanilla
    essence

Simmer the pumpkin in the water in a covered pan until the pumpkin is soft (about 20 minutes). Otherwise, put the pumpkin and water in a pressure cooker. Cover and bring up to pressure. Turn down heat and cook for 5 minutes then release pressure. Put pumpkin with juice into a liquidizer. Add the vanilla essence, honey and sugar and blend for 1 minute. Put the purée back into a pan (keeping back a little of the purée to mix with the arrowroot) and reheat. Add the arrowroot mixed with the reserved purée into the pan and bring to the boil, whisking all the time. Serve with any hot pudding such as crumble or with fruit salad.

Breakfast Suggestions

Breakfast is perhaps the easiest meal of the day for preparing nutritious and tasty vegan food. Muesli with fresh and/or dried fruit and toasted brown bread with vegetable margarine and tahini, honey or peanut butter will fill you up and provide you with an energy source that will last through the morning. In this section we have given a basic muesli recipe plus several other unusual breakfast ideas.

Note: There are more breakfast suggestions in the Children's Favourites chapter.

Muesli

Serves 1

This muesli recipe is the original kind of mixture that Dr Bircher-Benner (who invented muesli) intended people to eat as a healthy start to the day. It contains more fresh fruit than cereal.

- 1 large eating apple, coarsely grated
- 1 tablespoon porridge oats pre-soaked in 3 tablespoons (45 ml) cold water
- 1 teaspoon (5 ml) lemon juice
- 1 teaspoon honey *or* 3 chopped dates
- 1 tablespoon (15 ml) soya milk
- 1 tablespoon roasted and ground hazelnuts for topping

Mix all the ingredients, except the nuts, together. Top with nuts.

Variations
1. Soaked and chopped prunes instead of apple.
2. 1 teaspoon tahini with a little extra water (instead of soya milk) raises your calcium intake.
3. 1 tablespoon wheatgerm instead of nuts.

Hot Grapefruit
Serves 1

½ grapefruit
1 teaspoon or more honey *or*
  maple syrup

Prepare the grapefruit by running a sharp knife around the edge of the flesh and then along and down the segments. Top the grapefruit with honey or maple syrup and place it under a medium–high grill for about 5 minutes.

Nutty Breakfast Crunch
Serves 8

Store unused breakfast crunch in an airtight container. Serve it with a topping of chopped dates, raisins and fresh fruit.

3 oz (75g) vegetable margarine
1 teaspoon (5 ml) natural vanilla
  essence
1 tablespoon malt extract
8 oz (225g) porridge oats

2 oz (50g) chopped hazelnuts
2 oz (50g) chopped almonds
2 oz (50g) wheatgerm
2 oz (50g) sunflower seeds

Preheat the oven to 350°F (180°C, gas mark 4). Combine the margarine, vanilla and malt extract in a pan and gently melt the mixture. Mix this and all the other ingredients together. Spread the mixture onto a large baking sheet and bake for about 20 minutes in the preheated oven, stirring every 5 minutes. Remove from the oven and allow to cool.

Carrot and Almond Dish
Serves 1

Grated carrot is an unlikely breakfast food but this dish is delicious and particularly good for those on a weight-loss diet.

2 tablespoons wheatflakes
1 small carrot, grated
1 teaspoon (5 ml) lemon juice
1 tablespoon ground almonds

1 teaspoon honey
soya milk, diluted with the water,
  to taste

Put the wheatflakes in a bowl. Top with carrot and add the lemon juice. Sprinkle the almonds over the mixture, swirl with honey and add soya milk to taste.

Fruit Medley   *Serves 4*

This is a good winter breakfast starter and especially tasty in early spring when the first unforced rhubarb is available.

2 oz (50g) dried prunes, stoned and chopped
2 oz (50g) dried apricots, chopped
1 oz (25g) sultanas
1 stick rhubarb, chopped

1 teaspoon (5 ml) lemon juice
1 cooking apple, cored and chopped
creamed coconut, flaked, to garnish

Put all the ingredients in a saucepan, except for the coconut. Cover with water and cook for 20 minutes. Serve hot or cold, topped with flakes of creamed coconut.

Millet Porridge   *Serves 2*

This is a delicious change from oat porridge.

5 oz (150g) millet flakes
¾ pint (450 ml) water
soya milk to taste

dates or raisins to garnish
maple syrup to taste

Mix the millet flakes with half of the water in a saucepan. Add the rest of the water and cook until mixture thickens (about 12–15 minutes). Serve. Add soya milk with chopped dates or raisins and even maple syrup for a special sweet treat.

Variation:
For regular porridge substitute rolled oats for the millet flakes.

Apple Purée   *Serves 4*

Apple purée is refreshing on its own, cold, or as a hot topping over cereal.

1 lb (450g) dessert apples, cored and chopped
6 oz (175g) sultanas

grated rind of 1 lemon
½ teaspoon ground cinnamon
½ pint (275 ml) water

Put all the ingredients into a saucepan, bring to the boil, reduce heat and simmer, covered, for 10 minutes. Liquidize the mixture in a blender and serve it hot or cold.

Children's Favourites

After the savoury section, most of the sweet dishes use either honey
or the natural sugars found in fruit, dried fruit, nuts and seeds.
Children enjoy them and they are less likely to rot their teeth or set up
a chain-demand for more sugar than the many commercial sweets.
The recipes were collected by Claire, who has two small children.

Savoury Dishes

Baby's Butterbean Pudding   *Serves 1*

tablespoons cooked butterbeans
tablespoon wheatgerm
tablespoon grated carrot
tablespoon soya flour

½ teaspoon yeast extract
¼ teaspoon kelp powder
tomato juice

Mash the beans and mix them with the wheatgerm, carrot, soya flour,
yeast extract and kelp powder. Stir in enough tomato juice to make a
soft consistency. Transfer the mixture to a bowl, cover and steam for
10 minutes.

Walnut and Sunflower Roast   *Serves 4*

large onion, chopped
tablespoon (15 ml) sunflower oil
oz (225g) cooked millet
tablespoon tahini
tablespoon wheatgerm
teaspoon miso, dissolved in 1
tablespoon (15 ml) hot water

1 large carrot, grated
4 oz (100g) chopped walnuts
2 oz (50g) sunflower seeds
1 teaspoon (5 ml) soya sauce

Preheat oven to 375°F (190°C, gas mark 5). Sauté the onion in the oil in an ovenproof dish for 6–7 minutes over a low heat. Remove the dish from the heat and mix in the cooked millet, tahini, wheatgerm, miso, carrot and nuts and smooth the mixture flat. Mix the sunflower seeds with the soya sauce and sprinkle them over the top. Bake for 30 minutes in the hot oven.

Quick Peanut Butter Soup   *Serves 3–4*

Serve this soup with small crispy wholemeal rolls, spread with herb butter (pp. 76–7) if liked.

1 large onion, chopped
1 tablespoon (15 ml) vegetable oil
2 tablespoons (30 ml) tomato purée
1 tablespoon crunchy peanut butter
2 teaspoons yeast extract

1 pint (0·5 litre) vegetable stock *or*
  1 pint (0·5 litre) water with ½
  teaspoon yeast extract
chopped parsley to garnish

Sauté the onion in the oil in a large saucepan for 5 minutes. Add the tomato purée, peanut butter, yeast extract and stock. Bring the mixture to the boil, cover and simmer for 5 minutes. Serve garnished with chopped parsley.

Picture Salad

If your children aren't very keen on fruit and vegetables try making a picture with them. Our five-year-old loved trains so this is how we made his salad.

The secret is to use only ingredients you know they will eat, not the ones you would like them to eat. Later you can slowly introduce others. Let them make the pictures, too.

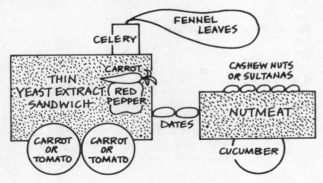

Sweet Dishes

Buckwheat Crêpes   *Makes 8 small pancakes*

3 oz (75g) wholemeal flour
1 oz (25g) buckwheat flour
1 tablespoon soya flour
salt to taste

8–10 fl oz (225–275 ml) water
a little vegetable oil for frying

Combine the flours and salt in a bowl. Mix in the cold water to form a medium-stiff batter. Beat the batter well and then leave it aside for 30 minutes. Beat the batter again and drop tablespoonful amounts into a small, oiled, hot frying pan. Turn when set and brown the underside. Serve on their own with honey and lemon juice or stuffed with grains, vegetables, leftover savoury dishes, etc.

Baby's Brown Rice Pudding   *Makes about ¾ pint (425 ml)*

This also makes an excellent breakfast and is delicious with any fruit in season such as pears or sieved blackberries.

2 oz (50g) sweet brown rice, ground
1 tablespoon ground almonds
½ pint (275 ml) diluted orange juice

2 oz (50g) fruit purée (apricots are ideal)
1 teaspoon tahini

Cook the rice and almonds in the orange juice over a low heat for 30 minutes. Stir in the fruit purée and tahini and serve warm.

Carob Brownies   *Makes 6 brownies*

4 oz (100g) wholemeal flour
1 tablespoon soya flour
1 oz (25g) carob flour
1 teaspoon baking powder
2 oz (50g) soft vegetable margarine

1 oz (25g) coarsely chopped walnuts
1 teaspoon (5 ml) vanilla essence
1–2 fl oz (25–50 ml) water to mix

Preheat oven to 350°F (180°C, gas mark 4). Combine the flours and baking powder and mix well together. Rub in the margarine. Mix in the walnuts. Mix the vanilla essence with the water and stir it into the flour mixture to form a soft dough. Put the dough into a greased shallow 6 in (15 cm) square baking tin and bake for 20 minutes in the hot oven. Remove the tin from the oven and cut the cake into square brownies. Leave to cool and then turn the brownies out of the tin.

Fruit Ginger Bars

Makes 12 oz (375g)

The bars are wrapped in rice paper and rolled out. Trim off excess rice paper. The rest sticks to the bars and makes them non-sticky.

8 oz (225g) dates
4 dried bananas
1 tablespoon preserved ginger
1 oz (25g) chopped walnuts
a little juice from the preserved
   ginger jar
1 teaspoon grated lemon peel
2 sheets of rice paper 7 × 11 in
   (17 × 27 cm)

ginger

Put all the ingredients through a mincer or blend together in a food processor or blender, adding more ginger juice if the mixture starts to stick. Spread the mixture down the middle of one of the sheets of rice paper, cover with the other piece and then roll it out to a thickness of about ½ in (12 mm). Trim off excess rice paper. Cut the slab into squares or bars, or into small squares as 'sweets' for children.

Carob 'Chocolate' Blancmange

Serves 4–6

8 fl oz (225 ml) soya milk diluted
   with 8 fl oz (225 ml) water
½ teaspoon agar agar
3 tablespoons carob flour

1 tablespoon honey
1 teaspoon (5 ml) natural vanilla
   essence

Put all the ingredients into a blender and liquidize for 1 minute. Transfer the contents of the blender to a small pan and bring the mixture to a gentle boil. Pour the boiling mixture into a blancmange mould. Transfer to a refrigerator or leave to cool in a cold place. The blancmange should be ready to eat in 4–5 hours.

Carob and Malt Fudge
Makes 6 oz (175g)

1 oz (25g) hard margarine
1 oz (25g) raisins, finely chopped
1 oz (25g) sunflower seeds, finely ground
1 oz (25g) malt extract

1 oz (25g) carob flour
1 oz (25g) rolled oats
1 teaspoon (5 ml) natural vanilla essence

Melt the margarine in a small pan and cook the raisins in it until soft (about 10 minutes). Stir in the sunflower seeds, malt extract, carob flour, oats and vanilla. Mix well and spread the mixture on a baking tray to a depth of ½ in (12 mm). Leave overnight in the fridge to set and cut into squares when cold.

Date Halva
Makes 10 oz (275g)

2 oz (50g) dates, finely chopped
2 oz (50g) raisins, finely chopped
2 oz (50g) tahini
2 oz (50g) soya flour

2 teaspoons finely grated orange rind
1 oz (25g) sesame seeds, roasted

Stir the dates and raisins into the tahini. Stir in the soya flour and orange rind and mix well. Shape the mixture into balls about ½–1 in (1–2.5 cm) diameter and roll them in the sesame seeds. Serve at room temperature or chilled.

Banana Delight
Serves 4

2 large bananas, sliced
1 tablespoon wheatgerm
1 tablespoon ground cashew nuts
2 tablespoons (30 ml) soya milk

juice of 1 orange
1 tablespoon (15 ml) concentrated apple juice

Put all the ingredients into a liquidizer and blend for about ½ minute. Distribute between four fruit bowls and serve.

Mock Banana Ice Cream
Serves 6

9 oz (250g) tofu, cut into 1 in (2.5 cm) cubes
4 large bananas, sliced

1 teaspoon (5 ml) lemon juice
3 tablespoons (45 ml) maple syrup

Put all the ingredients except the maple syrup into a liquidizer. Blend them together and distribute the mixture between four fruit bowls. Trickle maple syrup over the top of each to serve.

Fruit and Nut Bars *Makes 10 bars*

The bars are wrapped in rice paper which makes them non-sticky to hold.

1 oz (25g) soft vegetable margarine
6 oz (175g) dates, finely chopped
3 oz (75g) dried apricots, finely chopped
2 oz (50g) dried figs, finely chopped
3 oz (75g) dried bananas, finely chopped

grated rind of 1 orange
2 oz (50g) ground almonds
2 oz (50g) desiccated coconut
2 sheets rice paper 7 × 11 in (17 × 27 cm)

Melt the margarine in a pan over a low heat. Add the dates, apricots, figs, bananas and orange rind and cook them, stirring, for 5 minutes or until soft. Add the almonds and coconut, mix well and remove from the heat. Place the mixture down the middle of one of the pieces of rice paper and cover with the other piece of rice paper. Roll out with a rolling pin to flatten the mixture to a thickness of about ½ in (12 mm) and cut into bars. Trim off excess rice paper. Store unused bars in an airtight container.

Fruit and Sunflower Seed Bars *Makes 10 bars*

The bars are wrapped in rice paper which makes them non-sticky to hold.

4 oz (100g) raisins
4 oz (100g) dates
4 oz (100g) dried pears
4 oz (100g) sunflower seeds, ground
2 oz (50g) porridge oats

juice and grated rind of 1 lemon
2 teaspoons (10 ml) vanilla extract
2 fl oz (50 ml) cold water
2 sheets rice paper 7 × 11 in (17 × 27 cm)

Put the raisins, dates and dried pears through a mincer or grind them in a food processor or blender. Combine the mixture with the sunflower seeds, oats, lemon rind and mix well. Stir in the lemon juice, vanilla extract and water. Spread the mixture down the middle of one of the sheets of rice paper and put the other sheet on top. Roll out to a thickness of about ½ in (12 mm) and cut into bars. Store unused bars in an airtight container.

Carob Chews

Makes 15 chews

4 oz (100g) soft vegetable
  margarine
3 tablespoons honey

2 tablespoons carob flour
8 oz (225g) muesli
15 paper cake cases

Melt the margarine and honey in a pan over a low heat and stir in the carob flour. Bring the mixture to the boil and remove it from the heat. Stir in the muesli and drop spoonfuls of the mixture into the paper cases. Transfer the cases to the refrigerator and leave the carob chews to harden (about 1 hour).

Carob Chip Biscuits

Makes 24 biscuits

3 oz (75g) soft vegetable margarine
5 oz (125g) honey
6 oz (175g) wholemeal flour
1 tablespoon soya flour
2 teaspoons baking powder
4 oz (100g) chopped walnuts
4 oz (100g) sunflower seeds,
  roasted

2 fl oz (50 ml) water
1 teaspoon (5 ml) natural vanilla
  essence
4 oz (100g) soya-milk carob bar,
  cut into small chips

Preheat oven to 350°F (180°C, gas mark 4). Cream the margarine and honey together until light and fluffy (about 5 minutes). Add the flours, baking powder, walnuts and sunflower seeds and mix well. Stir in the water, vanilla essence and carob chips. Place spoonfuls of this mixture on a greased baking tray and bake for 10–15 minutes in the hot oven.

Peanut Butter Sweets

4 fl oz (100 ml) smooth *or* crunchy
  peanut butter
4 fl oz (100 ml) clear honey
1 teaspoon (5 ml) vanilla essence

6 oz (175g) heat-treated soya flour,
  e.g. Soyolk
toasted sesame seeds for rolling

Mix the peanut butter and honey together, then add the vanilla essence. Add the soya flour a little at a time, mixing first with a wooden spoon and then by kneading as with bread dough. Pinch off small amounts of the dough and roll these into little balls about ½ in (12 mm) in diameter. Roll the balls in the toasted sesame seeds. Put the sweets on a dish and set them aside in the refrigerator to harden (about 1 hour).

128

Sunny Smiles

4 oz (100g) porridge oats
2 oz (50g) barley flour
4 oz (100g) wholemeal flour
1 oz (25g) carob flour
1 tablespoon (15 ml) sunflower oil
1 tablespoon clear honey

1 teaspoon (5 ml) natural almond
  essence
concentrated apple juice to mix
a few sultanas and almonds to
  make faces

Preheat oven to 375°F (190°C, gas mark 5). Mix together the oats and flours. Stir in the oil, honey and almond essence and add enough apple juice to make a firm dough. Shape the dough into six balls and flatten them onto a greased baking tray. Bake them for 15 minutes in the hot oven. Remove them from the oven and make faces on them with the sultanas and almonds.

citrus fruit

Glossary

Most ingredients used in vegan cookery are familiar, everyday foods but there may be a few that are new to you. We hope we have included all the unrecognized ingredients in the following list.

Soya Bean Products

Miso A fermented soya bean and grain product, it has a thick consistency and is usually dark coloured with a pungent smell. Miso is rich in vitamins (including B12) and minerals and is good for settling the digestive system. It can be used in soups, stews, stocks, sauces, dressings, dips and spreads, but it is salty and care should be taken not to add extra salt. Miso keeps unrefrigerated for months.

Soya flour Special heat-treated soya-flour, such as Soyolk, can be used uncooked, e.g. in making vegan 'cheese'.

Soya milk This is made from boiled, crushed soya beans, and used by vegans in place of cow's milk. It is high in protein and low in fat. Soya milk is available commercially in health and wholefood stores. Buy fresh rather than canned milk (Plamil is a well-known brand) but, best of all, make your own. The following recipes are taken from the Vegan Society's booklet *Practical Veganism*, an excellent introduction to veganism.

Fresh Soya Milk   *Makes 2 pts (1·1 l) milk*

Rinse ¼ lb (100g) beans and soak them in 1 pint (0·5 l) water for ten hours or overnight. Wash well. Put the beans in a blender with very hot water, allowing about 1 pint (0·5 l) of water to 1 cup of beans. Blend well. Repeat until all the beans have been liquidized. Bring the liquid slowly to the boil in a large heavy saucepan, stirring frequently to prevent sticking. Watch it carefully because it will easily boil over.

Simmer gently for 20 minutes, stirring frequently. Line a colander with fine muslin and place the colander over a large pot or bowl. Pour or ladle the liquid into the muslin, catching the pulp in the cloth and the milk in the pot below. Twist the cloth tightly and use a wooden spoon to press on the bag to extract as much milk as possible. Rinse through any milk left in the pulp by re-opening the cloth, stirring in half a pint of boiling water, twisting and pressing again. Set the pulp aside (it is a useful base for soyaburgers and soysages). Cool the soya milk by placing the pot in a sink of cold water, and transfer it to covered containers for refrigerating or it will sour like cow's milk. It can be used in a variety of ways, but when drunk fresh most people prefer to sweeten it, perhaps with a little vanilla.

Quick Soyamilk   *Makes 2 pts (1·1 l) milk*

Blend 2 heaped tablespoons soya flour, 2 teaspoons sugar and 1½ pints (0·8 l) water for 15 seconds in a food processor. Add 4 fl oz (100 ml) oil and blend for a further 30 seconds. Bring the mixture to the boil over a high flame, then allow to cool. It will keep in a refrigerator for a week. Give it a thorough shake before use. It is good for cooking, in milk shakes and in cereals – but not in tea.

Soya sauce Made from soya beans and wheat, or just soya beans, natural soya sauce should have been aged for at least 18 months and it should be chemical free. Most soya sauce on sale is really a cocktail of chemicals and should not be used. Invest in a good brand or naturally aged shoyu (thinner and milder) or Tamari (thicker and stronger) soya sauce.

Tofu (also called beancurd) This is made by boiling soya beans, mashing the boiled beans through a sieve and collecting the liquid or milk, which is then set using a coagulant. Excess water is pressed off. Fresh tofu is best kept in water. Vacuum-packed tofu is also available. Tofu is rich in protein and minerals and low in fat. It is a versatile food and may be used in soups, stews, salads, dips, dressings or stir fried with vegetables. It may even be used in sweet dishes (cheesecake for instance) as a substitute for cheese.

Other Products

Agar agar This is a vegan gelatin made from seaweed and often used by vegans as a thickener in jellies, desserts, soups and stews.

Carob   The carob is a bean. It is nutritious, and when dried and ground into a flour is directly interchangeable with cocoa. It is used in place of chocolate (cocoa) – which contains caffeine – and needs no added sugar.

Molasses (treacle)   Sugar cane is processed and refined to obtain white sugar. The major residue of the process is molasses, which contains the vitamins and minerals sugar cane's original. Thus, as a sweetening agent, molasses is more nutritious than white sugar. It does, however, still contain natural sugar and it is not good for the teeth if left in contact with them. Molasses is much more strongly flavoured than sugar, naturally limiting the quantity used (which is not the case with refined sugar).

Tahini   A paste made from crushed sesame seeds, tahini is used to make spreads, bread dips, sauces and salad dressings. It has a creamy, nutty taste and is high in polyunsaturated fats.

Yeast extract   This is a savoury spread sometimes called brewer's yeast. Marmite is the best-known brand name. Some yeast extracts contain added vitamin B12. A list of good ones is available from the Vegan Society.

Conversion Tables

Conversion of Imperial Measurements to Metric

Weights		Liquids	
Imperial	Approximate metric equivalent	Imperial	Approximate metric equivalent
½ oz	15g	¼ teaspoon	1·25 ml
1 oz	25g	½ teaspoon	2.5 ml
2 oz	50g	1 teaspoon	5 ml
3 oz	75g	2 teaspoons	10 ml
4 oz	100g	1 tablespoon	15 ml
5 oz	150g	2 tablespoons	30 ml
6 oz	175g	3 tablespoons	45 ml
7 oz	200g	1 fl oz	25 ml
8 oz	225g	2 fl oz	50 ml
9 oz	250g	3 fl oz	75 ml
10 oz	275g	4 fl oz	100 ml
11 oz	300g	5 fl oz (¼ pint)	150 ml
12 oz	350g	6 fl oz	175 ml
13 oz	375g	7 fl oz	200 ml
14 oz	400g	8 fl oz	225 ml
15 oz	425g	9 fl oz	250 ml
1 lb	450g	10 fl oz (½ pint)	275 ml
2 lb	900g	15 fl oz (¾ pint)	450 ml
3 lb	1·4kg	20 fl oz (1 pint)	0·5 litre
		1¾ pints	1 litre
		2 pints	1·1 litres

Exact conversion: 1 oz = 28·35g

Oven temperatures

°F	°C	Gas mark
225	110	¼
250	130	½
275	140	1
300	150	2
325	170	3
350	180	4
375	190	5
400	200	6
425	220	7
450	230	8
475	240	9

Bibliography

Altman, N., *Eating for Life*, Theosophical Publishing House, 1973
Godlovitch, S. & R., and Harris, J., *Animals, Men and Morals*, Gollancz, 1971
Hall, R., *Voiceless Victims*, Wildwood House, 1984
Kapleau, R. P., *A Buddhist Case for Vegetarianism*, Rider, 1983
Linzy, A., *Animal Rights*, SCM Press, 1976
Regan, T., and Singer, P., *Animal Rights and Human Obligations*, Prentice-Hall, 1976
Singer, P., *Animal Liberation*, Cape, 1976
Wilson, F. A., *Food Fit for Humans*, Daniel Company, 1975
Wynne-Tyson, J., *The Civilized Alternative*, Centaur Press, 1972
Wynne-Tyson, J., *Food for a Future*, Centaur Press, 1975

Index